British Seaside Piers

Chris Mawson and Richard Riding

Ian Allan
PUBLISHING

First published 2008

ISBN (10) 0 7110 3251 3
ISBN (13) 978 0 7110 3251 4

© Chris Mawson and Richard Riding 2008

Published by Ian Allan Publishing

an imprint of Ian Allan Publishing Ltd, Hersham, Surrey, KT12 4RG
Printed in England by Ian Allan Printing Ltd, Hersham, Surrey, KT12 4RG

Code: 0804/B

Visit the Ian Allan Publishing website at www.ianallanpublishing.com

Front Cover photograph: Eastbourne Pier. (*English Heritage*)

Title Page photograph: Rhyl Pier in 1935. (*English Heritage*)

This book is dedicated to the memory of Cyril Murrell (1898-1958, *pictured right*) who took many of the vintage aerial
photographs used in this book.

British Seaside Piers is not intended to be a definitive history of piers, far from it. Nor indeed is it a guidebook of piers in their present state. As can be seen within this book, even within the limited space available, the history of individual piers is often cyclical in nature with periods of prosperity, decline, and for the luckier ones, rejuvenation. At the time of writing, several of Britain's better-known piers are closed and inaccessible to the public, awaiting repair or restoration. This partly explains why we have chosen to illustrate our seaside piers in their glorious heyday without modern photographs that can date overnight.

Firstly, a note about the choice of piers in this book. Following years of debate that is still ongoing, the National Piers Society (NPS) settled on a list of some 55 existing piers that are classed as 'traditional pier structures'. This may sound like a small number as Britain's coastline is studded with numerous manmade constructions which jut out to sea. However, most of these structures – including a number of Scottish 'piers' – are classed as jetties, harbour walls and so on. Despite the NPS's definitive list, some of the piers featured in this book have been viewed as questionable. The absence of amusements has convinced some that Hythe Pier is not a 'pleasure pier' as such. Similarly, the 'pavilion on stilts' form of Weymouth Bandstand and Burnham-on-Sea piers seems very far removed from the classic designs of piers as seen in Brighton or Eastbourne. One suspects the 'when is a pier not a pier' debate will continue for some time.

As can be seen in this book, there were 90 piers in the UK, of which around 50 are open and fully functioning. Over 30 have disappeared and one of the most exciting aspects of researching this book has been tracking down aerial views of some of the 'lost' piers, many of which have not been published before. Some were found almost by accident, such as the 1920 view of Rhos Pier, for which the glass plate negative was misfiled in an envelope marked Colwyn Bay.

Having stated that this book is not a definitive history, it would be churlish to deny the reader a brief historical overview. There is some disagreement as to the first 'commercial' or 'pleasure' pier. It is possible that the earliest pier evolved from a pre-existing landing stage at Margate, which in 1808 offered a promenade and bandstand following partial rebuilding. However, the first purpose-built pier was constructed at Ryde on the Isle of Wight and opened in July 1814. This was followed by two chain or suspension piers at Leith in Edinburgh and on the Sussex coast at Brighton in 1821 and 1823 respectively. Whilst elegant to look at, chain piers were prone to storm damage and only one further chain pier was built, at Seaview on the Isle of Wight, which by 1898 was the only one of its type remaining.

These early piers were built to provide two essential functions. Firstly they allowed paying visitors the opportunity to promenade along the pier, to experience the closest thing to walking on water. As John Betjeman wrote, 'A pier is about the only place left in any town where walking is possible without having to look back all the time for oncoming vehicles. It also provides a walk on the sea without the

ABOVE: Ryde Pier is generally regarded as Britain's first pleasure pier. The original 1740ft structure took just a year to build and was opened on 26 July 1814. *(Richard Riding collection)*

disadvantage of being seasick.' The other important function for piers was to provide landing stages at their seaward ends for paddle steamers, which offered inexpensive but elegant excursions between coastal towns and ports. Fleets were based chiefly around the south coast of England, and it is no coincidence that this part of the country also saw the building of a great many piers. For early pier operators, their chief source of income came from either end of the pier: from pedestrian visitor tolls and steamer landing dues. It was only later that they sought to develop commercially the parts of the pier that linked the two.

By 1860, a further 11 piers had been erected, mostly along the south and east coasts of England. Of these early piers, only three remain at Ryde, Lowestoft (South) and Great Yarmouth (Wellington). After 1860 however, a veritable boom in pier building began, which continued well into the first decade of the 20th century. Of the 90 piers featured in this book, nearly 70 were built in the 40 years between 1860 and 1900. Many were funded by speculative companies that could offer shareholders rewards in terms of dividends and protection in the eventuality of financial failure, thanks to the newly created status of Limited Liability.

INTRODUCTION

ABOVE: Shanklin Pier before and after the 1987 storms that destroyed much of the structure. The remains were demolished in 1993. (*Environment Agency*)

Most were successful, but a handful suffered from poor financing including Shanklin Pier, which opened in 1890 but was put into the hands of receivers just two years later. Investors in piers were not solely out for profit. Many were looking to put their town on the rapidly developing holiday map of Britain, and the arrival of a pier helped transform otherwise undistinguished coastal towns such as Blackpool into the popular resorts they were to become.

While piers were being built at a prolific rate, a number of the earlier piers were succumbing to neglect and the ravages of nature. In the final quarter of the 19th century, storm damage led to the demise of the first pier at Walton-on-the-Naze (1881), Cowes Royal (1882), Brighton Chain (1896) and Leith Trinity Chain the following year. Elsewhere, collisions with drifting sailing ships led to the eventual demolition of Hornsea Pier in 1897 and Coatham Pier in 1899. As can be seen in this book, the various threats from wind, waves, shipping and conflict would impact on nearly every pier in this book at one time or another.

Whilst a few piers were deteriorating, others were evolving. Decks were widened, shops, kiosks and bandstands were introduced, and at Blackpool North Pier in the mid-1870s, a new 'Indian Pavilion' was built, the first of its type. By the end of the century, such pavilions were becoming an increasingly common sight, and formed part of the pier's evolution from a simple promenade pier (or glorified landing stage) into the 'pleasure pier'. By the Edwardian period, the most multi-functional piers could offer daily concerts, sideshows, 'fancy diving', other aquatic displays and a host of other entertainments. In some towns, such as Brighton and Blackpool, these developments were the manifestation of competition between piers. At other single pier resorts they were designed to draw day-trippers from neighbouring towns along the coast. That such additions could be made was testimony to the durability and adaptability of these piers' cast-iron substructures. By contrast, some of the piers that were destroyed in the 1890s were chiefly built of timber.

Mention should be made of Eugenius Birch (1818-1884), naval architect, engineer and pier builder who designed some 14 piers from 1855 to 1884, including Blackpool North, Eastbourne, Hastings and Weston Birnbeck. At Brighton's West Pier, Birch's nephew carried on the work of his uncle, designing the 125ft long pavilion that opened in 1893, and remains today in skeletal form following its destruction by fire in 2003. Fewer than half of the Birch piers survive complete, and of these, many have been significantly altered. Another notable engineer was James Brunlees, whose designs include some of the longest British piers at Southend and Southport, as well as Llandudno, arguably one of the least altered of all Victorian piers.

The Edwardian period marked a high point in the popularity of piers, although financially some suffered to the point that they had to be taken over by their local municipal authority as at Southend, Great Yarmouth, Bournemouth and neighbouring Boscombe. The last pier to be built before the advent of the Great War was Fleetwood in 1910, and the next completely new pier, Weymouth Bandstand, would not be built until 1939. One would have expected the Great War to have stopped pier development in its tracks, but in a few cases it continued, as at Brighton West Pier where the oval Concert Hall was opened in 1916. The only pier to suffer as a direct result of the war was Ramsgate Marina in 1918, when a drifting mine exploded beneath, causing extensive damage.

The period from 1919-1939, when many of the aerial photographs in this book date from, provided mixed fortunes for Britain's piers. Several were demolished, including Dover (1927) and Ramsgate Marina (1930) whilst others faced the threat of fire. It is depressing to recall, but many of the piers in this book have suffered fires at one point or another, the most recent (at the time of writing) being Southend in 2005. The fine pavilion at Weston Grand was destroyed in 1930, as was that at Worthing in 1933, but both were swiftly rebuilt. Elsewhere, 'pleasure' piers were evolving further to become funfair or amusement piers. At Clacton, the shoreward end was dramatically expanded to accommodate a dance hall, casino, swimming pool and rollercoaster ride. Between 1927 and 1937, Brighton's West Pier saw the addition of a miniature racetrack, mirror maze and amusement arcade, all introduced in order to boost visitor numbers.

All was to change with the advent of World War 2. Most piers were closed within months of the outbreak of war and suffered the indignity of being breached, with entire sections being removed to prevent them forming convenient landing stages for invading enemy forces. While Minehead was the only pier to be demolished for military reasons, others suffered damage from mines, bombs and resulting fires; Southsea Clarence Pier was destroyed by bombing in January 1941. By 1945, many were in a dire state of disrepair, though there was no immediate rush to demolish piers after the end of hostilities. Most piers were restored, as shown by the 1947 aerial photos of Swanage and Boscombe that are published here. However, by the advent of the 1950s, several piers had become so dilapidated that demolition became the only option; St Leonards, Seaview Chain, Plymouth and Folkestone had all been dismantled by 1954. Indeed, since 1950, some 17 seaside piers have been demolished, whilst a further three can no longer be viewed as viable or traditional pier structures. With the notable exception of Brighton's West Pier, no piers have been lost since the demolition of those at Ventnor and Shanklin in 1993. That said, many piers suffered during the second half of the 20th century, especially when the package holiday began to lure increasing numbers of British holidaymakers away from their native beaches to warmer and more exotic locations.

Since the creation of the Heritage Lottery Fund in 1994, the climate surrounding historic buildings has changed. The fund's existence means that restoration is at least equal to the option of closure and/or demolition, a choice that was not open to the pier owners of the early 1950s, for example. That said, a number of piers remain closed and in a state of inevitable, though not irreversible, decay.

Today, piers can be broadly classified into one of four broad groups or types. The first comprise those piers that offer a limited (some might argue tasteful) range of facilities to the visitor, often a long promenade, shelters, kiosks and perhaps a landing stage. These piers are found chiefly in Wales, southwest England and the Isle of Wight and include Bangor, Swanage, Clevedon and Totland Bay. At the other end of the spectrum are those that offer the full-on pier experience such as Clacton, Brighton and Blackpool Central. Somewhere in between these extremes are the smaller piers that offer the full range of traditional pier attractions, but usually on a reduced scale. Piers in this group include Worthing, Cromer, Sandown and the country's one and only 21st century pier at Southwold.

To one side of the above groupings are those piers that are, to a varying degree, shadows of their former selves. These often had their pavilions or amusements at the shoreward end, and decay or neglect of the neck and led to these being

ABOVE: Brighton West Pier photographed from a height of just 80 feet *circa* 1919. *(Richard Riding collection)*

demolished, either fully or partially. This has left a number of piers consisting of a pavilion near the shore and little else, as seen at Fleetwood, Cleethorpes, Herne Bay and Aberystwyth.

Perhaps this is an apt point to explain the choice of photos for this book, as those looking for photos of piers in their current state may be disappointed. Whilst we were keen to make the best of Ian Allan's impressive in-house eight-colour printing presses, the majority of the photos herein are black and white, and chiefly date from the late Victorian age through to the 1950s. Yes, piers are colourful, even garish subjects for the camera, whilst abandoned piers offer possibilities for more artistic photography. By contrast, we wanted to show them in their heyday, and in the case of the aerial shots, from a viewpoint rarely seen in previous pier books.

From the 1890s onwards, piers were extremely popular subjects for postcard publishers and in a similar way, they caught the attention of early commercial aerial photographers, many of them ex-RFC personnel forging new careers after the end of World War 1. A good example is the low altitude shot of Brighton West Pier taken in 1919, the chopped-off foreground suggesting the cameraman still had much to learn about the medium. The 1913 photo of the isolated Worthing Pier (on page 117) must be one of the earliest air-view postcards in existence, dating from a time when aerial cameras were in their infancy. Many of the aerial photos in this book were taken during the 1920s and 1930s, an era when photographers were using bulky glass plate cameras whilst being buffeted around in the open cockpits of biplanes such as the De Havilland DH9 – that the results could be pin sharp is a testament to their skill and in-flight resilience.

One largely forgotten photographer of this period was Cyril Murrell, who began his career with Aerofilms in the mid-1920s before setting up his own company, Aero Pictorial Ltd., in 1934. Murrell was clearly attracted to photographing seafronts and piers in particular, and just a fortnight before the outbreak of World War 2, he took dozens of photos along England's south coast, sensing that it might be the last chance to photograph this vulnerable area. Piers photographed by Murrell on these sorties and reproduced here include Bournemouth, Paignton, Ryde, Sandown, Shanklin, Southsea Clarence and Teignmouth. As it happened, all these piers survived the war, although Murrell had already photographed many others such as at Plymouth and St Leonard's that would have disappeared by the mid-1950s. Something of a loner within his field, Cyril Murrell died in 1958 aged 59 and this book is dedicated to his memory.

The outlook for Britain's seaside piers in the 21st century depends on where you are standing – literally. For some piers such as Brighton Palace, the future is encouraging. However, for the neighbouring West Pier, things would appear terminal. Joining it on the critical list are those long-closed piers such as Weston Birnbeck and Ramsey Queens where the will to restore exists, though not the funding as yet. But we should not paint too bleak a picture, and need reminding that in the era of national lottery funding more seems possible than, say, 20 years ago. Yes, a number of high-profile restoration schemes have been refused funding, but at least some of Britain's piers have benefited from lottery grants.

Above all, our seaside piers need patronage, most of all from visitors who enjoy their many attractions, and in doing so put money into those all important coffers. If nothing else we hope this book encourages this to happen, even if the reader is spurred on merely by curiosity to see how much the piers have changed since the photos reproduced here were taken!

ABOVE: This evocative photo shows a paddle steamer approaching Bournemouth Pier on 20 August 1939, just two weeks before the outbreak of World War 2. *(English Heritage)*

Aberystwyth's Royal Pier, on the shores of Cardigan Bay, was the first purpose-built pleasure pier in Wales. Designed by Eugenius Birch and built by J. E. Dowson during 1864-1865, the 800ft pier was opened on Good Friday, 1865. During the first day, 7000 visitors paid to walk the boards but this promising start was frustrated when a severe storm washed away a 100ft section of the pier in January the following year. It was not until 1872, following a change of ownership, that the pier fully recovered from this setback.

In July 1896, the Princess of Wales opened a 3000-seat pavilion, designed by G. Croydon Marks and built at a cost of £8,500. In November 1938, another storm caused extensive damage, reducing the pier's length by half. By the early 1970s, the structure had deteriorated to such an extent that the pier neck was closed to the public. Following acquisition by Don Leisure Ltd in 1979, the pier was modernised and improved during the following decade. A snooker club and restaurant were added in 1987. Around this time, planning permission was granted to build a new pier alongside the existing one but nothing became of it.

In 1990, a nightclub with the name Pier Pressure was opened as well as an Indian restaurant at the far end of the pier that played host every year to the town's Indian food festival. Only 300ft of the original 800ft structure remains today. At the time of writing, there are a few amenities including an amusement arcade, café/restaurant and bar.

LEFT: Edwardian postcard view of Aberystwyth Pier, showing the pavilion opened in July 1896. Built in a mixture of styles, it featured three aisles surmounted by domed glass roofs. In the 1920s, the pavilion was converted into a cinema. *(Richard Riding collection)*

LEFT: This aerial view of the pier was taken in 1947, by which time the structure had diminished to less than half of its original length. *(English Heritage)*

BELOW: Seen from sea level, this view of Aberystwyth Pier was probably taken during the Royal Navy's visit to the town in 1911. The ship's crew can be seen arriving in smaller boats and climbing the boarding steps at the end of the pier. *(Richard Riding collection)*

BANGOR GARTH 1896

Designed by John James Webster of Westminster and built by Alfred Thorne, Bangor Garth's 1550ft pier, costing £14,500, was opened on 14 May 1896 by Lord Penrhyn. Featuring a pontoon landing stage at its head, the pier was built specifically for operating the Garth ferry across the Menai Straits but could also receive steam ships from the Isle of Man, Blackpool and Liverpool. Because of its long length, it featured a baggage line, though this was removed after the coaster SS *Christina* – ironically carrying building material for the pier from Liverpool – collided with the structure in 1914. The resulting gap in the pier was temporarily bridged and was not repaired until the early 1920s.

By 1971, the pier had become dangerous and was closed to the public. In 1974, the borough council sought approval to dismantle the pier but their proposal was defeated by a single vote. Plans went ahead to save the pier, which by now had been awarded Grade II listed status. In 1975, it was sold for the nominal sum of 1p to Bangor City Council on condition that it was repaired and reopened to the public. Funding for the restoration came from the Welsh Development Agency, the Historic Buildings Council for Wales and the Heritage Memorial Trust. Following a five-year building programme, the Marquis of Anglesey officially reopened it on 7 May 1988. Today, Bangor Garth is regarded by many as one of Britain's finest and least-altered Victorian piers, and one which could have disappeared had it not been for the tenacity of Jean Christie, Bangor's Mayor at the time the pier changed hands in the mid-1970s.

RIGHT: A near-vertical aerial photograph of the pier, taken in 2005. The design of the pier is broadly similar to that at Llandudno, built some 20 years earlier. (*Royal Commission for Ancient and Historical Monuments for Wales*)

BELOW: The pier extends two-thirds of the way across the Menai Straits. (*Richard Riding collection*)

BANGOR. THE PIER.

Opened in 1846, this pier was constructed in two sections: stone nearer the shore and iron at the seaward end. The pier suffered from storm damage in 1872 and had to be rebuilt. In 1895, it was extended to 570ft and a 2ft 6in gauge hand-operated baggage rail was laid along the western side of the wooden deck to serve the steamers operated by the Liverpool & North Wales Steamship Company. A T-head landing stage was added for this purpose.

Towards the end of the 19th century, a small pavilion was constructed on the seaward end of the pier. It is unclear when this was removed but it is certainly still in evidence in the 1947 aerial photo (left). After the war, there was a downturn in passenger services, and when the pier's landing stage becoming unsafe, it was dismantled. During the 1960s, the pier was restored at a cost of £15,000. Ownership of the pier passed to the Isle of Anglesey Council in 1974, since when further repairs have been carried out. Today, Beaumaris Pier is the home of the Blue Peter II lifeboat station, sited alongside the main deck.

ABOVE: A classic Edwardian view of Beaumaris Pier with a carriage in the foreground and a steamer at the landing stage. *(Richard Riding collection)*
LEFT: An aerial view of Beaumaris Pier taken in 1947. *(English Heritage)*
BELOW: A view showing the lost seaward end pavilion. *(Richard Riding collection)*

BLACKPOOL NORTH 1863

The North Pier, the first of Blackpool's three piers, was designed by Eugenius Birch and officially opened on 21 May 1863 by the chairman of the Blackpool Pier Company. After a landing jetty was added in 1864 and extended in 1867, the pier ran to some 1650ft in length. With the acquisition of paddle steamers *Clifton* and *Queen of the Bay*, the pier company ran frequent services to the Isle of Man, Llandudno, Southport and Liverpool.

Blackpool North was one of the first piers to see significant commercial development in the mid-Victorian period. In 1874, an Indian pavilion was added to the pier head along with a bandstand, shops and a restaurant. Further extensions took place in 1875 and 1877 when electricity was installed. £5000 of damage was caused when it was struck by the Norwegian barque *Sirene* in 1892, and in 1897, Nelson's former flagship HMS *Foudroyant* was wrecked whilst moored by the pier during an exhibition. The Indian pavilion was gutted in September 1921 and its replacement was also destroyed by fire in 1938. A new 1500-seat pavilion built on the site in 1939 survives.

During 1986-1987, the entrance buildings were rebuilt in Victorian style at a cost of £350,000. The storms of 1987 severely damaged the seaward end jetty. In 1990, helicopter flights from the jetty were introduced from this Grade II listed pier, and in 1991, a new tramway and carousel bar were opened. The pier is currently owned by Leisure Parcs and is regarded as the most 'traditional' of Blackpool's three piers.

TOP LEFT: The second pavilion ablaze on 19 June 1938, in a photo taken from Blackpool Tower. Its successor, built in 1939, still stands today. *(Richard Riding collection)*
LEFT: A hand-tinted Edwardian postcard view of the pier. The trams in the foreground are advertising Tennents lager and Munich beer. *(Richard Riding collection)*
OPPOSITE: An aerial view of the pier taken in July 1955. *(English Heritage)*

BLACKPOOL CENTRAL 1868

Originally named the South Pier, Blackpool's Central Pier was opened on 30 May 1868 with little pomp or ceremony. Designed by John Isaac Mawson, the 1518ft structure included a 400ft low-water jetty and cost £10,000 to build. At first business was poor until the introduction of cheap steamer excursions in 1870. With the addition of games and open-air dancing (the North Pier did not permit dancing) 'The People's Pier' never looked back, though the steamer trade slackened off during the inter-war period and ceased in 1939.

The pier entrance was altered in 1877 and again in 1903 with the addition of the White Pavilion. After the adjacent Victoria ('South') Pier was opened in 1893, the pier's name was changed to Blackpool Central. At the turn of the 20th century, there was a nationwide craze for roller-skating and the pier's owners were not slow in pandering to this, opening a rink in 1909. Soon after a joy wheel was introduced; speedboats and car racing were added in 1920.

The 1903 shore end White Pavilion was demolished in 1966 and was replaced by the Dixieland Palace and Golden Goose, opening a year later at a cost of £15,000. Though damaged by fire in 1973, the Palace was rebuilt and later served as an arcade and nightclub. During the gales of 8 December 1974, the jetty was damaged and later demolished, reducing the pier's length to 1118ft.

Following acquisition of all three Blackpool piers in the 1980s by First Leisure Plc, the Central Pier underwent a £4 million redevelopment programme, which included construction of a two-storey arcade, the Wheelhouse Bar and the spectacular 108ft high Ferris Big Wheel. Built in Holland and opened for Easter 1990, the wheel can accommodate up to 216 passengers and its construction necessitated the strengthening of the pier's substructure. Currently owned by Leisure Parcs, this pier offers all the latest in traditional amusements.

TOP RIGHT: A between-the-wars view showing a busy Central Pier.
(Richard Riding collection)
RIGHT: This aerial view of the pier was taken in July 1955. *(English Heritage)*

TOP: An Edwardian postcard view of Blackpool's Central Pier, c1900.
(*Richard Riding collection*)

ABOVE: An Edwardian view showing the pier entrance and White Pavilion.
(*Richard Riding collection*)

RIGHT: The pier pictured from the air in July 1965, shortly before the White Pavilion was demolished. Note the narrow low water jetty, which was dismantled in the mid-1970s.
(*English Heritage*)

Often described as 'The Unwanted Pier', there was great opposition by the upmarket locals to Blackpool's third pier when plans were announced in 1890. They feared the structure would interrupt their view of the sea and attract the kind of clientele that would adversely affect property values – an early example of NIMBY-ism. A compromise was reached and building of the pier began in August 1892. The opening of Blackpool's shortest pier took place amidst the strains of a 50-piece orchestra, two brass bands and a choir on Good Friday, 31 March 1893. Interestingly, vague plans followed for two further piers in Blackpool, though these never got past the drawing board.

Designed by T. P. Worthington, the 492ft Victoria Pier – renamed 'South' Pier in 1930 – was built of iron and steel and cost £50,000. The piles were driven into the ground using the Worthington Screwpile System, where pressurised water was forced down the centre of the pile to loosen the sand until the required depth had been reached. Once the sand retracted the piles were firmly held in place. The 3,000-seat Grand Pavilion, designed by John Dent Harker of Manchester, was opened on 20 May the same year. Originally more upmarket than its sister piers, the South Pier featured more than 30 shops, a bandstand and a resident orchestra of 40 players. The pier offered other amusements, some of which must have offended the sensitivities of some of the more sniffy locals, such as a boxing kangaroo, a bird warbler and a hypnotist. From 1901, the pier offered cinematic entertainment.

In 1938, the pier entrance was widened and the Regal Pavilion was built. The pier survived the war, and although it had been more fortunate than its neighbours with regards to storms, the post-war period was bedevilled with fires. The Grand Pavilion was destroyed by fire in 1964 and was replaced barely three months later by the Rainbow Theatre. This survived until 1998 when it was demolished to make way for a £1.5 million rollercoaster, the Crazy Mouse, and a group of bungee-type rides within the appropriately named Adrenalin Zone.

ABOVE: An aerial view of the much-altered South Pier taken in 1976.
(English Heritage)
RIGHT: An Edwardian postcard view of the 'Victoria' Pier and the South Shore.
(Richard Riding collection)
LEFT: The interior of the Flora Hall on Blackpool South Pier shot in the 1930s. Seats were free except for Sunday evenings and special concerts.
(Richard Riding collection)
OPPOSITE: A dramatic head-on aerial photograph of the pier taken in July 1920. Most of the pier buildings seen here had disappeared by the 1960s.
(English Heritage)

BOGNOR REGIS 1865

Bognor Regis Pier was designed by Joseph W. Wilson who went on to design the piers at Hunstanton and Teignmouth. Costing £5,000 to build, the simple 1000ft structure was bereft of buildings and was officially opened on 4 May 1865. One night in January 1867, the pier was damaged when the sloop *Nancy* slipped her moorings and several supporting columns were swept away. The pier soon began to lose money and plans were laid to have the structure dismantled and moved elsewhere. Once local ratepayers got wind of this, the pier was purchased for £1,200 by the local council in December 1876.

Over the next 30 years, the pier was improved and extended. A bandstand was added in 1880, followed by a pavilion at the seaward end in 1900. Despite this, by 1908 the pier was deteriorating and the town council sold it to the Bognor Pier Company for 10s 6d (52p). Things started to improve after the pier's shore end was widened from 18ft to 80ft in 1910-1911. This enabled the building of a huge new complex that housed a restaurant, cinema, arcade and 1400-seat theatre. Around this time, a roller-skating rink occupied the entire length of the pier. The development of the pier was completed in 1936 when a three-tier landing stage was added, allowing steamers and motorboats to berth just off the seaward end.

Bognor Pier saw action in both world wars, with some 200 servicemen billeted there between 1914-1918, whilst during World War 2, it was temporarily renamed HMS *Patricia* (some say *Barbara*) and used as a Royal Navy observation station. The pier was restored in 1947, but since then it has suffered a long decline in fortunes. The seaward end pavilion was damaged during severe storms in November 1964, and on the night of 3-4 March 1965, it sank into the sea following a blizzard. In December 1974, the pier was closed following two fires

ABOVE: This aerial view of the pier was taken in 1959 and shows sunbathers and divers on the landing stage. *(English Heritage)*

within three months. Despite having become a Grade II listed building in 1989, this offered no protection when in January 1990, the new pavilion was damaged by a storm. The century ended on a similarly gloomy note when 60ft of decking was washed away from the seaward end on 24 October 1999.

In 1996, a £25 million futuristic scheme was unveiled to build a new 1000ft pier with a pyramid-shaped building at the shore end, dubbed The Pieramid and designed by Bognor cartoonist Mike Jupp from an original idea by Steve Goodheart. The 50-metre high structure was to have been constructed in bronze and glass and its interior would have housed a National Seaside Heritage Centre. Although supported by West Sussex and Arun Councils, the Millennium Commission turned down the plan.

Today, Bognor Regis Pier is best known for its annual International Bognor Birdman Rally held each summer. This competition was originally staged in 1971 at nearby Selsey but was transferred to Bognor Pier in 1978. Competing for a £25,000 prize, contestants are required to glide 100 metres in homemade contraptions, and although the prize has not yet been won, the resultant publicity has put Bognor Regis firmly on the map.

ABOVE: A view of the pier c1914 with charabancs by the roadside and bathing machines at the water's edge. *(Richard Riding collection)*

OPPOSITE: This aerial photograph was taken in 1932 before the addition of the three-tier landing stage. *(English Heritage)*

In a gesture of independence and a symbol of rivalry with nearby Bournemouth, Boscombe embarked upon constructing its own pier in 1888. Designed by local architect Archibald Smith, who had been responsible for nearby Southbourne Pier, work was carried out by the Waterloo Foundry of Poole. Built in less than a year, the simple 600ft long pier was opened on 29 July 1889 by the Duke of Argyll. The new pier proved a disappointing attraction and was acquired by Bournemouth Corporation in 1904. Improved facilities and attractions were added in an effort to attract more visitors, including the exhibition for several years of the skeleton of a 65ft whale washed up on a nearby beach in January 1897!

Despite its improvements, the pier fared no better and by the 1920s, the structure was in need of repair. During 1924-1927, the head was renewed in high alumina concrete, noted for its strength and quick-setting properties. Boscombe pier was one of the first marine structures to make use of this material and the renovation increased the pier's length to 750ft. In 1940, in company with many other piers, Boscombe was breached to deter invaders but was repaired during the late 1940s (see the aerial photograph opposite).

During 1958-1960, the neck was rebuilt whilst the entrance building was replaced, the result being that almost the entire pier was built of concrete of one form or another. At the pier head, a restaurant and the Mermaid Theatre were added, though the latter never operated as such, being first used as a covered ice skating rink before being converted to an amusement arcade from 1965. By the 1980s, the pier's structure was deteriorating and consultants warned that the pier head could collapse in 'extreme continuous storm conditions'. There were also large cracks appearing in the reinforced steel used in some of the concrete piles. During the pier's centenary year, work was carried out on the wooden deck, but in April 1990, the pier had to be temporarily closed to the public. During the ensuing years the pier was well patronised with free entry although the pier head and the theatre remained closed.

In 2003, Bournemouth Council announced exciting plans for the pier. One ambitious £9 million redevelopment scheme was to demolish the structurally unsafe pier head and add a new pavilion-style entrance that would embody a restaurant with panoramic views, amusements and family attractions. All these grandiose plans came under threat when the pier's entrance building, dating from the 1958-1960 reconstruction and likened to a glorified concrete bus shelter, was suddenly given Grade II listed building status, which means it cannot be demolished. This unremarkable building retains its four kiosks with their original 1950s shop fronts and lettering! At the seaward end of the pier, the Mermaid Theatre and the landing platform have been demolished and replaced with a smaller open platform. An artificial reef for surfing is planned east of the pier.

TOP: An aerial view of the much-altered pier in 1963, showing the streamlined 1950s entrance building. *(English Heritage)*
ABOVE: A between-the-wars view showing the original entrance building. *(Richard Riding collection)*
OPPOSITE: This fascinating aerial photograph of the sectioned pier taken in 1947 shows repair and re-decking work in progress. A temporary landing stage leads out from the beach to receive boats whilst the pier is closed. The inter-war entrance building still retains elements of its predecessor, such as the ornamental turrets poking through the flat roof. *(English Heritage)*

BOURNEMOUTH 1880

Today's pier at Bournemouth is the third one to be built on the site. The first was a 100ft wooden jetty for receiving steamers. Completed in August 1856, it was replaced five years later with a 1000ft wooden pier designed by George Rennie. Despite the wooden piles being replaced with cast-iron in 1866, a severe storm in January the following year all but washed the structure away, completely destroying the T-shaped head. Following another storm in 1876, the pier was no longer suitable for receiving steamers and was demolished. A temporary landing stage was built whilst Eugenius Birch set about designing a new 838ft iron pier.

Opened on 11 August 1880 and costing £21,600, the new pier featured a two-storey Indo-Gothic style pavilion. Additional buildings including bandstands and wind shelters were added in 1885, and extensions to the pier were made in 1894 and 1909, taking the total length of the structure to 1000ft. With the opening of nearby Southbourne and Boscombe piers in 1888 and 1889 respectively, the Bournemouth area boasted three piers along a six-mile stretch of the coast. By the mid-1890s, only two other towns could lay claim to having three piers: Blackpool and Brighton. Bournemouth Pier's landing stage provided berths for four steamers at a time and gave a real boost to the town. During the 1901 August Bank Holiday alone, ten steamers brought 10,000 trippers to the pier.

In the spring of 1940, Bournemouth beach was closed to the public and the pier was breached by the army as a defence measure, remaining closed until August 1946. From 1947-1950, the pier head was completely reconstructed, though it had to be renewed in 1960 in order to support the new pier theatre. By 1976, the

ABOVE: An Edwardian postcard view of Bournemouth Pier showing the Indo-Gothic entrance pavilion. *(Richard Riding collection)*
RIGHT: Three paddle steamers moored at Bournemouth Pier's landing stage in 1937. *(English Heritage)*

pier had deteriorated badly and a rebuilding and refurbishing programme costing £1.7 million was completed in 1981. By this time, the pier bore little resemblance to Birch's original structure, the charming entrance building replaced by a two-storey octagonal Disney-style amusement arcade. Other facilities included shops and a circular café affording wonderful views looking across the water to the Isle of Purbeck.

On 13 August 1993, the IRA's attempt to further modify the pier with an incendiary bomb attack failed, only causing minor damage. On the same day, a more serious and substantial explosive device was found strapped to a girder under the pier. It is believed that it had been primed to explode the previous evening when 800 people had gathered to watch a performance of *Don't Dress for Dinner* in the pier theatre. Thankfully, it failed to explode and the device was removed. In 1996, Bournemouth Council announced plans to erect a hi-tech 21st century pier to take the resort into the next millennium at a cost of £13 million. During 2000, the landing stage was replaced in sections to combat worn piles and rising sea levels due to the effect of global warming.

LEFT: This 1947 aerial view shows the pier during the course of reconstruction following the wartime breaching. *(English Heritage)*
BELOW: A recent view of Bournemouth Pier *(Anthony Wills)*.

BRIGHTON PALACE 1889

For a brief period, Brighton had no fewer than three piers, albeit in various stages of construction and destruction. The Chain Pier was in its final death throes and the West Pier had been established for 30 years when work began on the Palace Pier during the mid-1890s. After the formation of the Palace Pier Company in 1886, work began on Richard St. George Moore's design in November 1891; however, its construction did not run smoothly. The original contractors barely lasted a year, and in 1895 work stopped due to lack of funds – at this point, the pier had reached a length of 1060ft.

The uncompleted pier was opened to the public on 20 May 1899 by the Mayoress of Brighton whilst work continued on the pier head and theatre, which took the pier to its finished length of 1760ft. Supported on 368 cast-iron screw piles, the original pier was fairly plain except for triple arches placed at intervals along the decking outlined in electric lights. The ornate pier head theatre was opened on 3 April 1901, later enlarged to seat 1500. In 1910-1911, the pier was developed further with the addition of a pavilion and winter garden at the shoreward end, a full-length central windbreak and an extensive steamer landing stage.

The pier was the subject of numerous precautionary measures during World War 1. A lookout was posted at the pier head whilst sentries patrolled the deck at night. Sandbags were placed along the rails and mines wired in readiness to demolish sections of the pier in the event of an invasion. During the 1930s, the seafront promenade was widened and the pier entrance had to be moved back about 40ft, during which time the canopy and clock tower were added. In 1934,

RIGHT: An aerial view of the Palace Pier taken in 1947, shortly after it was repaired and reopened after the war. *(English Heritage)*
BELOW: Edwardian holidaymakers at play. *(Richard Riding collection)*

a number of toll boxes from the Chain Pier were re-sited on the Palace Pier. During 1937-1938, the east pavilion was erected and the pier extended.

During the evacuation of Dunkirk in May 1940, the pier was requisitioned and the theatre closed. The central portion of the pier was blown up by the army and heavily mined. Although the Luftwaffe made several attempts to bomb the structure, none were successful, and in early 1946, the pier was derequisitioned, repaired and reopened to the public on 6 June 1946. By 1970, much of the piling under the landing stage had deteriorated despite earlier repair work, and the decision was taken to demolish it. As this work was being carried out, a drifting Thames barge loaded with scrap iron caused £1 million worth of damage to the pier head.

After a change of ownership, the theatre was dismantled in 1986 and a large pleasure dome erected in its place. For over 30 years, this has been the town's one and only functioning pier, therefore it has been renamed Brighton Pier. Presently owned by the Noble Organisation, and offering a huge range of attractions, it looks set for a long and profitable future.

RIGHT: An aerial view of Brighton Palace Pier taken in September 1935. *(English Heritage)*
BELOW: The pier pictured in the 1930s. *(Richard Riding collection)*

BRIGHTON WEST 1866

Rarely does a pier make national headlines but Brighton's West Pier, Britain's only Grade I listed pier, did just that in 2002-2003. Regarded by many as Eugenius Birch's finest pier, Brighton West was opened on 6 October 1866. Components for the pier had to be shipped from Scotland and were erected by R. Laidlaw & Sons of Glasgow. By the time of the opening, the cost had escalated and the pier company had been dissolved and then reincorporated with increased capital.

Built on slender iron columns attached to piles screwed into the chalk seabed, the 1,115ft pier was 50ft wide and was designed for promenading, though initially it was a simple structure without amusements. At first, inadequate cross-bracing caused movement of the columns, which alarmed the promenaders, though this problem was soon rectified. After Napoleon III inspected the pier in 1870, he said it was Britain's finest structure. The pier was to become very popular, and by the middle of the 1880s, was attracting a million visitors a year, prompting a move to add more amenities to amuse and entertain. During 1893, the pier was lengthened and widened and an oriental pavilion designed by Birch's nephew Peregrine Birch was opened on 19 October of the same year. In an effort to attract more visitors by sea, a landing stage was built in 1896 and enlarged in 1901, by which time electricity had reached the pier. By now, what had been a 'promenade pier' had evolved into a 'pleasure pier'.

Unsurprisingly, the number of visitors dropped during World War 1, in which time, the concert hall midway along the pier's neck was opened in 1916. After 1918, visitor numbers reached an all-time high of two million plus, but as these figures declined, further attractions were added including a miniature race track, amusement arcade and bathing station. At the start of World War 2, the pier remained in use, but during May 1940, it was requisitioned by the military. After the landing stages were mined and depth charges laid, the structure was breached between the pier head and the concert hall by the Royal Engineers. In the autumn of 1943, the mines were removed and at the war's end, the 60ft breach was plugged. The pier was partially reopened to the public on 18 April 1946 and fully operational by early 1948. By this time, many changes had taken place; no longer a pleasure pier, it had virtually been turned into an offshore funfair. By the late 1950s, there was a marked decline in visitor numbers and little in the way of new attractions, though the pier continued to profit well into the next decade. During 1969, it was the principal location for Richard Attenborough's film *Oh! What a Lovely War*.

The pier's long and final decline began in 1970 when the pier head was sealed off from the public as being unsafe. In September 1975, the rest of the pier was closed, 109 years after its opening. In 1978, the West Pier Trust, consisting of a

TOP RIGHT: An aerial photograph of the pier taken in 1949, showing extensive post-war repairs still underway. *(English Heritage)*

RIGHT: An early engraving of Brighton West Pier. *(Richard Riding collection)*

group that wanted to save the structure, purchased the pier from the Crown Estate Commissioners for the nominal sum of £1,000. For 25 years, the pier stood abandoned, memorably likened to a 'drowning chandelier', whilst conservationists and English Heritage endlessly discussed its future, hampered by legal challenges. The pier became completely detached from land when the decaying shoreward end was dismantled in 1991. Hopes rose for a full restoration in 1998 when Heritage Lottery funding of more than £14 million was secured, but further delays followed. In December 2002, the partial collapse of the concert hall dealt a mortal blow to the very concept of restoring the pier. By this point, estimates for restoration had reached £30 million – a sum that appeared increasingly unrealistic to investors. On 28 March 2003, fire gutted the pavilion, and six weeks later, a similar fate befell the remains of the concert hall, confirming suspicions that arsonists were to blame. Today, the pier consists of little more than the twisted metal work of the iron frame pier head and pavilion. Lottery funding has been withdrawn, and at the time of writing, it is doubtful that restoration of this historic pier is ever likely to happen.

RIGHT: An aerial view of the deteriorating West Pier taken in 1998. Note the steel walkways, which allowed limited numbers of visitors onto the pier. *(English Heritage)*
BELOW: The burnt-out pier pictured in June 2004. *(Fred Gray)*

British Seaside Piers

Entrepreneur and railway engineer Peter Schuyler Bruff (1812-1900), known as the 'Brunel of the Eastern Counties', already had interests in nearby Walton-on-the-Naze, Felixstowe and Harwich when he acquired a large parcel of farmland at Clacton in 1864. Bruff had visions of turning the sparsely populated area into a limited high-class development resort for the middle and upper classes. One of Bruff's first engineering priorities was to build a pier and railway line from Clacton to nearby Thorpe-le-Soken in 1882.

Although sanctioned by parliament in 1865, work on the 480ft pier did not commence until 1870. At first little more than a landing stage, the wooden structure was 12ft wide and was officially opened on 27 July 1871. This was good timing because 5 August was to be the nation's first ever Bank Holiday when the working population had a day off. In 1878, a lifeboat station was added to the pier and the town's first lifeboat, *Albert Edward*, was officially launched on 10 July. In July 1882, Bruff's Clacton railway was finally opened, reducing the journey time to London in 90 minutes, as opposed to the five-hour trip by steamer. The hurriedly built pier was too short for steamers to berth at low tide, therefore the structure was lengthened to 1180ft and a new landing stage added during 1890-1893. The pier head was of an unusual polygon shape with a two-storey iron-framed pavilion with a balcony.

Between 1897 and 1915, the pier was owned by the Coast Development Corporation Ltd, which also owned several other piers and operated seven Belle steamers along the east coast. After the company went into liquidation, local entrepreneur Ernest Kingsman stepped in during 1921 and acquired all assets, including Clacton Pier. He then sold everything but the pier, for which he had ambitious plans.

With the steamer trade in decline, Kingsman turned his attention to transforming Clacton Pier into an amusement centre rather than a glorified landing stage. The Kingsman family formed the Clacton Pier Company, and between 1922 and 1934, £200,000 was spent on its development. This included the addition of the famous Blue Lagoon dance hall, the Crystal Casino, an open-air swimming pool (billed as the only pool in the world built over the sea), three theatres and a zoo. Clacton Pier is renowned for reinventing itself, and under the Kingsmans, its entertainments and amusements were ever changing to suit the tastes of succeeding generations. From 1937, the Steel Stella coaster dominated the Clacton skyline. The opening of a Butlins holiday camp in 1938 attracted even more visitors to the pier, and then came the war.

Before the pier was breached as an anti-invasion measure, a floating mine badly damaged the structure in February 1940. Clacton was declared a no-go area and the influx of visitors was restricted and not relaxed until August 1944. By this time, the Children's Theatre and the Crystal Casino had been demolished. After the war, the pier was repaired and it was business as usual, though it was never to be on the scale of the Golden Thirties. With the advent of cheap overseas holidays,

visitors to Clacton diminished, a situation that was not helped by the highly publicised troubles between Mods and Rockers over Easter 1964, when many families decided to give Clacton a miss.

In 1971, the Kingsmans finally sold the pier after which it slowly fell into decline. A fire in 1973 destroyed the Steel Stella roller coaster, and five years later the 50-year old Ocean Theatre was closed. A series of storms in 1978, 1979 and 1987 all took their toll. After another change of ownership in 1994, Clacton Pier is back in business and the site is billed as 'the largest undercover fairground in East Anglia'.

BELOW: An aerial view of the pier taken in July 1932, before the addition of the Steel Stella roller-coaster. *(English Heritage)*
OPPOSITE: An aerial view of Clacton Pier taken in 1964. *(English Heritage)*

CLEETHORPES PIER 1873

Financed by the Manchester, Sheffield & Lincolnshire Railway Company (MS&LRC – later LNER), Cleethorpes' 1,200ft pier was constructed for £8,000 and opened on August Bank Holiday in 1873. In 1884, the MS&LRC took over the lease of the pier, and in 1888, a concert hall was built at the pier head, only to be destroyed by fire in 1903. Its replacement was erected halfway along the pier whilst a café and shops were built on the site of the first building. By this time, the pier had been purchased by the LNER, who sold it back to Cleethorpes Council in 1936, after which the elevated link to the adjoining pier gardens was removed.

In 1940, the pier was breached as a defence measure, and in 1949, the seaward end of the structure had to be demolished following storm damage. Because of insufficient funding the pier remained truncated, its length reduced to 335ft. It still retained the pavilion and this was updated and extended to become a 600-seat concert hall, complete with café and bar. The pavilion received another facelift in 1968 to the tune of £80,000 and offered a variety of entertainments. By 1980, the pier was suffering heavy losses and the council sold the structure for £55,000 to Funworld Ltd, a Skegness-based company. The company wanted to develop the foreshore along with the pier, but when this idea was turned down, they sought to sell the pier back to the council. When the council showed no interest in the pier, it was threatened with demolition. However, in July 1985, the pier was purchased by businessman and nightclub owner Mark Mayer, who immediately spent £300,000 on converting the pavilion into a nightclub, complete with restaurant and games room. Renamed Pier 39 after the old San Francisco steamer pier of the same name, it reopened for business on 4 September 1985. Since then, successive owners have spent well over £1 million on developing the pier.

In 1999, proposals were put forward by the Cleethorpes Tourism Forum for a brand-new pier sited at the northern promenade and the extension of the existing pier to its original 1,200ft length, but they failed to materialise. In 2002, Pier 39 was forced to close on account of poor hygiene standards and owners, Luminar Leisure, undertook another costly facelift. On 18 September 2003, the pier was reopened and features two dance rooms. It is currently owned by businessman Kash Pungi.

ABOVE: This aerial view of Cleethorpes Pier was taken in May 1930, showing its original length of 1,200ft. *(English Heritage)*

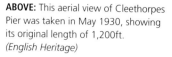

OPPOSITE: Aerial view of Cleethorpes and its truncated pier taken on a busy Bank Holiday weekend in May 1953. *(English Heritage)*

Interior of Pier Pavilion, Cleethorpes.

LEFT: An Edwardian postcard view of the full-length pier showing the second (surviving) pavilion. *(Richard Riding collection)*

FAR LEFT: The interior view of the pavilion, a barrel-vaulted structure with little ornamentation. *(Richard Riding collection)*

CLEVEDON 1869

Richard J. Ward and John William Grover were responsible for designing one of the country's most elegant piers – the late Sir John Betjeman likened it to "a Whistler oil sketch or a Japanese print." Plans were first mooted in 1829 but it was not until 1863 that an Act of Parliament for a pier was passed. In 1866, the town was offered a second-hand pier for £6,000 by the Aberystwyth Pier Company, but this 800ft structure, originally ordered by a foreign customer, was considered too narrow and plans went ahead for an entirely new pier.

Work began in 1867 and it took a workforce averaging 60 men and 15 months to complete the pier. The structure consisted of eight 100ft spans of wrought-iron girders made from modified Barlow railway lines carried on wrought-iron columns and screw piles. The structure has a 180ft masonry approach, and because of the famous Severn tidal range, the 842ft long pier was carried on 48ft high legs. After the pier was officially opened in March 1869, it enjoyed financial success but by 1890, a downturn in visitors and rumours that the structure was unsafe prompted the shareholders to offer it to the council. In the event, Sir Edmund Elton, the main shareholder, purchased all shares and gave the pier to the town in 1891.

The original pier head was rebuilt in cast-iron, and in 1894, McDowell & Stevens of the Melton Ironworks erected a Japanese-style pavilion in the same material. A storm in January 1899 washed away a stretch of decking from the area of the tollhouse, and in 1910, a new wooden landing stage was wrecked by another gale. The replacement structure, made from ferro-concrete, was opened in April 1913.

As early as 1952, there were concerns about the strength of the structure that led to regular bi-annual checks being carried out; in 1948, cast-iron trestles had been added to support the first span. On 17 October 1970, during a load test, the pier was declared unsafe after the two outer-most spans and 200ft of decking collapsed, unable to bear the required load of 50lb per square foot. The pier was closed to the public just a year after marking its centenary.

During the following year, the structure was Grade II listed and the Clevedon Pier Preservation Trust was set up in 1972 to help raise funds for a full restoration. Within a few years, the estimated cost of restoration had risen ten-fold, and in July 1979, the council declared its intention to have the pier demolished. After a public enquiry in March 1980, the demolition order was withdrawn and, following a costly structural survey, restoration of the pier neck took place between 1985 and 1988.

After the pier had reopened in May 1989, a lottery grant enabled full restoration of the entire structure to begin in 1997. This work, costing £3.2 million, was soon completed and the pier was reopened on 23 May 1998 by Sir Charles Elton, the great-great-grandson of the chairman of the original Clevedon Pier Company.

Voted Pier of the Year by the NPS, 1999

ABOVE: An aerial view of the pier taken after the collapse of two spans following load tests in October 1970. *(English Heritage)*
LEFT: An Edwardian postcard view of Clevedon's elegant pier. *(Richard Riding collection)*
OPPOSITE: An aerial view taken in August 1928. *(English Heritage)*

ABOVE: This aerial view was taken in 1962. Most of the pier seen here dates from the 1933-1934 rebuilding. *(English Heritage)*

LEFT: The disastrous fire of 1922, which totally destroyed the pavilion. *(Richard Riding collection)*

FAR LEFT: An Edwardian postcard view of Colwyn Bay Victoria Pier and original pavilion. *(Richard Riding collection)*

OPPOSITE: An aerial view of the pier taken in 1920, showing the pavilion and smaller bijou pavilion at the seaward end. *(English Heritage)*

COLWYN BAY VICTORIA 1900

No doubt spurred into action following nearby Rhos-on-Sea's acquisition of a second-hand pier from the Isle of Man in 1895, work on a new pier at Colwyn Bay began in 1899. Designed by the Manchester-based engineering firm Mangnall & Littlewood, the building of the pier was carried out by the Widnes Iron Foundry in two phases. Of traditional construction, the pier was made from prefabricated parts enabling rapid assembly. The wooden decking was supported on steel girders and cast-iron columns. Work was completed in 12 months and the pier opened on 1 June 1900.

What it lacked in length was more than compensated for by the pier's splendid five-domed 2500-seat pavilion, which in no small part helped to make the whole venture a success; so much so that the second stage of development was put into action during 1903-1904, when the structure was extended to 766ft. Unlike the piers at Rhos-on-Sea and Llandudno, Colwyn Bay Pier did not feature a landing stage.

In 1916, the 600-seat bijou pavilion was opened at the seaward end of the pier. Between the wars, the pier was plagued by destructive fires. The first wiped out the main pavilion in 1922 and its loss was a financial disaster for the Victoria Pier Company, forcing it to sell the pier to the local council. A replacement was opened the following year, but in 1933, both this and the bijou pavilion burned down within weeks of each other (shades of Brighton West 70 years later). The replacement pier, prudently constructed of concrete, was officially opened on 8 May 1934 at a cost of £45,000.

Owing to its location well away from the threat of invasion, the pier escaped being breached during World War 2. Business on the pier thrived throughout the 1950s, but with the disbanding of the once popular orchestra in 1962, it faced hard times and was acquired from the council by Trust House Forte in 1968. The pier became a Grade II listed building in 1975, and during the following year, the owners declared their intention to demolish the seaward end of the pier. This action was not carried out and the pier passed to Parker Leisure Holdings, who allowed the non-profitable seaward end to deteriorate to the point where it became unsafe. Even the elements conspired to rid the pier of its seaward end when a gale caused damage in 1987. After much wrangling, the council agreed that the failing part of the pier could be demolished, which prompted the formation of the Victoria Pier Action Group to prevent such action. Following the purchase of the pier in 1994 by Mike and Anne Paxman, who wanted to retain the entire pier, a pier trust was set up in 1999 in order to purchase it from them. (The Paxmans lived on the pier as a condition of their building insurance policy because they could not afford the cost of professional security.) In a bizarre twist, in 2003 the pier became the first – and quite possibly last – to be auctioned on eBay, and on 31 December was acquired by Steve Hunt, who announced his intention to embark upon a three-phase restoration programme.

COWES VICTORIA 1902-1961

In keeping with the rest of Britain, the seaside resorts of the Isle of Wight were not slow in providing piers to encourage the multitude of excursion steamers that plied the south coast during the second half of the 19th century. Cowes, ideally placed to take maximum advantage of the Solent traffic, produced three piers. The first was Fountain Pier, actually a stone quay that projected about 60ft to accept steam packets. With the opening of the Royal Pier in 1867, Cowes had a fashionable promenade pier, even though it was too short to receive steamers at low tide. The 250ft wooden structure had a landing stage and featured a 50ft high pagoda, ballroom and refreshment bars. In September 1876, a storm, described as a tornado, devastated Cowes and damaged the Royal Pier beyond repair. It was to be 25 years before the town's third pier materialised.

During the intervening years, the lucrative excursion trade had bypassed Cowes as the town lacked a suitable berthing place for larger vessels. Designed by R. E. Cooper, construction of the new pier was entrusted to Alfred Thorne of Westminster, who had been responsible for those at Shanklin, Dover and Cromer. The simple 170ft long pier, considered to be 'more useful than ornamental', featured a cast-iron shank with a pier head on timber piles and cost £7,379. The pier was officially opened in March 1902 and adopted the name Victoria as a tribute to the late queen who had made regular visits to her beloved Osborne House to the east of Cowes. The pier prospered and during its first year 100,000 people made use of it.

During World War 1, the pier was used for the movement of troops. Similarly on the outbreak of World War 2, the pier was taken over by the Royal Navy. After the war, the pier was in a state of disrepair and had suffered from fire damage. Because of the post-war recession there was no money available for restoration, and after the pavilion was demolished in 1951, the pier passed into private ownership in 1960. Although the new owner had attempted to restore the pier, it had been more or less dismantled by the end of 1961.

TOP RIGHT: The entrance to Victoria Pier, Cowes c.1908. *(Richard Riding collection)*
RIGHT: Cowes Victoria Pier pictured during Regatta week in the 1920s. The pavilion was added in 1904. *(Richard Riding collection)*
OPPOSITE: An aerial view of Cowes Victoria Pier taken in 1938. *(English Heritage)*

Prior to the present pier's construction in 1900-1901, several jetties and piers had served Cromer from as far back as the 14th century. In August 1846, a new wooden pier with sloping piles costing £995 was opened, only to be badly damaged by the brig *Marsingale* on 19 December 1854. Although repaired, the pier fell victim to a storm in 1897 and was finally removed the following year.

The current pier was designed by W. T. Douglas & Arnott of Westminster and built by Alfred Thorne. The 450ft structure, including the slipway, was opened by Lord Claud Hamilton on 8 June 1901. The total cost of construction is stated to have been £18,000. During 1905, a shelter at the pier head was roofed over to form a pavilion; the work was carried out by Boulton & Paul of Norwich at a cost of £1,800. Further improvements were made to the 1,000-seat pavilion in 1921. On 26 July 1923, a lifeboat house was opened to house the *H F Bailey*, taking the pier's length to 500ft. On the outbreak of war in 1939, the pier was closed to the public. In July 1940, the pier's centre section was blown up as an invasion precaution leaving the lifeboat station marooned at the seaward end. To enable access, planking was laid across the gap making the lifeboat crew's work hazardous even before they launched their boat!

After the war, the Hunstanton Pier Company briefly acquired the pier before it was taken over by Cromer Urban District Council in 1948. Repairs amounting to £90,000 were undertaken and on 9 June 1951, on the occasion of the pier's 50th anniversary, the structure was reopened by HM Lieutenant of Norfolk Sir Edmund Bacon. During the severe storms that hit the east coast in January 1953, the pier and its pavilion were damaged; a pile leg snapped, deck furniture dislodged and concrete slabs that replaced the wooden decking had lifted.

In 1974, ownership of the pier was transferred to North Norfolk District Council, and in 1976, the structure was listed as a building of historical and architectural importance. On 26 February 1990, severe gales lifted the pier's amusement arcade, which was dumped 300 yards along the beach. Shortly afterwards, the pier was repainted and steelwork renovated at a cost of £500,000. Then, as luck would have it, a storm in February 1993 caused damage to the pier, mostly to the decking. On 14 November the same year, the construction rig *Tayjack* crashed through the pier and isolated the theatre and lifeboat station. The 36-metre breach was repaired and the pier was reopened on 1 May 1994 by the Rt. Hon. Mrs Gillian Shepherd MP.

During 1996-1997, the lifeboat station was demolished and a replacement was opened in 1998. This spotless building houses the RNLB's Tyne Class lifeboat *Ruby and Arthur Reed II*. This traditional pier's theatre runs highly successful summer shows and is well worth a visit.

LEFT: An aerial view of the pier taken in July 1932, showing the lifeboat house and slipway opened in 1923. *(English Heritage)*
OPPOSITE: This aerial photograph of Cromer Pier was taken in 1920, before the addition of the lifeboat house and slipway. *(English Heritage)*

There has been a pier at Deal in Kent since 1838, but the present pier is unique in that it is the only completely new pier built in Britain since World War 2. John Rennie was responsible for the town's first pier, erected in 1838 for the Deal Pier Company at a cost of £12,000, though only 250ft of the planned 445ft length was completed after the company ran out of money. Before too long, the pier suffered from sandworm and the ravages of storms, the worst of which destroyed the structure in 1857.

After the formation of the Deal & Walmer Pier Company in September 1861, Eugenius Birch was engaged to design the town's second pier. Contractors Laidlaw began work on the 1100ft structure in 1863 and local MP Mr. Knatchbull-Hugessen opened the uncompleted pier on 14 July 1864. Supported on wrought cast-iron columns, it featured a three-decked pier head, seating along its entire length and a landing stage for steamers. Because of its great length, a tramway was laid for carrying goods and baggage. Unfortunately, there were insufficient funds to pay the contractor and ownership was transferred to R. Laidlaw the following year. A restroom was added in the 1870s and a pavilion was opened on the pier head in 1886.

On 19 January 1873, the barque *Merle* struck the pier during a storm, and on 26 January 1884, a similar incident befell the schooner *Alliance*; repairs being made following both accidents. In 1920, Deal Borough Council acquired the pier for £10,000, but 20 years later disaster struck. On 29 January 1940, the Dutch vessel *Nora* was struck by a mine whilst anchored offshore. Against local advice, the wrecked craft was towed to the shore and beached, partly submerged. As the tide came in, the *Nora* was repeatedly thrown against the pier until she eventually

crashed through the structure causing 200ft of the decking to collapse. No less a personage than Winston Churchill gave consent for the army to demolish the remains of the pier to enable coastal guns a clear line of fire. All that remained were the tollhouses.

For the next decade and a half, Deal was without a pier; however, in 1954, Concrete Piling Ltd started work on a new pier to the design of Sir William Halcrow & Partners. The reinforced concrete structure, including the decking, is 1,026ft in length. The pier featured an arrow-shaped three-decked landing stage, but a miscalculation in the design resulted in the lower deck being permanently

BELOW: This aerial view of Deal's second pier was taken in September 1937. *(English Heritage)*

BOTTOM LEFT: An Edwardian postcard view of the same pier. *(Richard Riding collection)*

covered by the sea! It was opened by the Duke of Edinburgh on 19 November 1957 and entered in the history books as the first standard-length seaside pleasure pier to be built in Britain since 1910. Internationally acclaimed by anglers, ownership of the pier was taken over by Dover District Council. During the 1990s, this comparatively young pier was already showing signs of deterioration leading to a £3 million restoration programme between 2002 and 2004.

ABOVE AND ABOVE LEFT: Aerial views of Deal's third and current pier taken c.1958. *(Both: English Heritage)*

LEFT: The twisted remains of Deal Pier following the unwanted attentions of the Dutch vessel *Nora* in January 1940. *(Richard Riding collection)*

PROMENADE PIER, DOVER

COPYRIGHT 3416

The local town council turned down original plans for a pleasure pier at Dover in 1881. However, a pier company was formed in 1888, and on 22 May 1893, the Dover Promenade Pier was officially opened. Engineered by John James Webster, who went on to design the piers at Bangor Garth (1896) and Minehead (1901), Dover Promenade was constructed by Alfred Thorne at a cost of £24,000. Like that at Bangor, Dover Promenade Pier was notable for its Moorish-style kiosks at the entrance and along the pier neck. Within months of the pier's opening, the vessel *Christine* collided with the 900ft structure, and a year later, in November 1894, a 100ft stretch of the pier's central section was swept away in a series of gales. Such was the severity of the damage along the coast that it was reported in the *New York Times*. The pier was closed for repair for nine months and reopened in August 1895.

In 1901, a pavilion designed by of W. J. Alcock was added at the seaward end. Paddle steamers ran excursions to London and the pier was visited by steamers on the regular Margate to Folkestone service. Additional attractions included 'Professor Davenport', a diver who jumped into the sea in a sack! Despite these efforts, as early as 1903 it was clear the pier was not a great commercial success, with additional funds being raised to keep it solvent.

In 1911, the pier was leased to local businessman Robert Forsyth, who had successfully taken on the lease of Folkestone's Victoria Pier in 1907. However, before he could make an impact, the Admiralty purchased the pier for landing use in 1913, being renamed The Naval Pier. After World War 1, it was leased as a pleasure pier once more, but gradually fell into disrepair. By 1926, with the cost of restoration proving prohibitive, the pier was closed on the orders of the Admiralty. The pier's superstructure was sold off by auction and the remains demolished during 1927.

Two other piers at Dover are still in use today, though neither is a pleasure pier and therefore technically out of the scope of this book. Dover Admiralty Pier was completed in 1851 to receive cross-Channel steamers. Dover Prince of Wales, now owned by the Dover Harbour Board, was completed in May 1902 and had a railway running along its length. Both piers are popular with anglers.

TOP LEFT: An early view of Dover Promenade Pier. *(Richard Riding collection)*
LEFT: This postcard view from the pier towards the shore is postmarked 4 June 1903. *(Richard Riding collection)*
OPPOSITE: An aerial view of Dover's Promenade Pier taken in 1920. *(English Heritage)*

EASTBOURNE 1870

Eastbourne's pier is generally regarded as one of Eugenius Birch's finest. The protracted construction of this 1000ft pier was entrusted to J. E. Dowson, who died before the pier was completed. The work, undertaken by Head Wrightson of Stockton, began in April 1866. On 13 June 1870, Lord Edward Cavendish of Devonshire opened the half-completed structure. The pier was not finished until 1872. On New Year's Day 1877, the pier's entire shore end was washed away by a storm. Eugenius Birch carried out the necessary repairs, the new structure being built to a higher level. Visitors should look out for the incline towards the seaward end, past the blue room.

In 1888, a 400-seat theatre was built, later replaced with a 1000-seat building during 1899-1901; the earlier structure was removed in one piece to Lewes to become a cowshed! In 1893, a three-berth landing stage was added to the pier and extended in 1912. In 1925, a 900-seat music pavilion was built at the shore end at a cost of £15,000. It later served as a ballroom before becoming an amusement arcade in 1968. At the beginning of World War 2, army sappers breached the pier and machine guns were installed in the camera obscura – a Bofors gun was positioned at the shore end. The pier narrowly escaped destruction when a mine detonated near the shore end; the resulting explosion pushed the blue room two feet to one side. The pier was strafed a number of times by the Luftwaffe as Eastbourne was the victim of many hit-and-run raiders.

In 1951, the second entrance building was replaced with the now characteristic kidney-shaped structure. In 1968, the pier was purchased by Trust House Forte, and in 1970, an employee nearly succeeded where the Germans had failed when he set fire to the pier's theatre. This was subsequently rebuilt as the Dixieland Showbar, but the camera obscura was not replaced for another 33 years. The pier gained a new arcade in 1985 as part of a £250,000 clean up. In October 1987, the landing stage was wrecked by a gale. Between November 1990 and April 1991, a new £500,000 entrance building was built by WFC of Devon and opened on 15 June 1991 by the Duke of Devonshire. During 2003, a camera obscura was restored to the pier after a gap of over 30 years. Housed in a tower approached via a spiral staircase, the lens projects a rotating 360-degree panorama of Eastbourne seafront and the English Channel onto a curved screen.

Voted Pier of the Year by the NPS, 1997

RIGHT: Taken in 1946, this aerial photograph of the pier shows post-war repairs to the neck still in progress. (*English Heritage*)

Cornwall's only pleasure pier is located at Falmouth and currently plays host to 400,000 visitors each year. The modest 300ft structure was built during 1903-1905, the foundation stone being laid by the Prince of Wales – later to be King George V. Traditional booths are located at the entrance and the uncluttered deck has occasional seating and ornamental lamp standards. The pier was repaired and modernised in 1951 when six boat transfer staircases and all-weather shelters were added. It was at this pier that the survivors of the successful British attack on the heavily defended docks of St Nazaire in occupied France on 28 March 1942 returned to port, five days after the flotilla had left Falmouth. The pier is also much used by night fishermen for pollock, mackerel and flounder. The pier's royal connections continued on 1 May 2002 when HM Queen Elizabeth II began her Golden Jubilee tour of her kingdom, landing at the pier.

TOP: The pier in 1913 with the steamer *Alexandra* in the foreground. Note the horse-drawn delivery carts. *(Richard Riding collection)*
ABOVE: A 1930s view of Falmouth Prince of Wales. *(Richard Riding collection)*
LEFT: An aerial photograph of the pier taken in June 1928. *(English Heritage)*

FELIXSTOWE 1905

The 'new pier' at Felixstowe was the last to be built by the Coastal Development Company (CDC), the company that owned Belle Steamers and built several other piers including Southwold and Lowestoft Claremont. Completed in 1905 and engineered by Rogers Bros., the pier's length of 2640ft necessitated a 3ft 6in gauge electric tramway to be laid along the north side. Though not completed, the pier was opened on 1 July 1905. After the CDC was wound up in 1922, ownership passed to East Coast Piers Ltd.

At the outbreak of World War 2, the tramway service was suspended and the pier was breached as a defence measure. After the war, the tramway remained closed and over three-quarters of the pier neck was demolished at the seaward end. Today, the pier is only 450ft in length and has an amusement building at the shore end. In 1997, a £2.5 million plan to refurbish the pier was announced; it was estimated that £750,000 was required just to prevent the structure from crumbling into the sea. Sadly these plans have been shelved due to lack of funding and the pier's long-term future is in jeopardy.

ABOVE: A paddle steamer approaches the Felixstowe landing stage. *(Richard Riding collection)*

RIGHT: An aerial view of the shortened pier taken in June 1954. *(English Heritage)*

Roughly midway between Morecambe and Blackpool, Fleetwood seemed an ideal location for a new pier, though plans drawn up in 1892 were rejected. It was not until 1909 that the go-ahead was finally given and the new pier was opened on Whit Monday 1910 to the design of G. T. Lumb. Costing £30,000, the 492ft pier was initially a plain structure with a landing stage and a few amusements at the shore end. This changed with the addition of a pavilion in 1911, but plans to further extend the pier came to nothing. As a result, the pier remained unchanged until the 1930s when minor improvements were carried out, followed by the addition of a small cinema in 1942.

The pier survived the war unscathed though re-decking was necessary in 1946. However, on 25 August 1952, a devastating fire virtually wrecked the pier. Almost completely rebuilt, the 'new super pier' opened to business the following year. In 1972, the pier received a £70,000 facelift, and during the late 1980s, further redevelopment took place including the rebuilding of the Jolly Roger Bar, later renamed Jollies Bar. A new café facility was opened at the front of the pier. During 1990, the pier's neck was closed following storm damage – the seats forming the sides to the first section of the neck were blown from one side to the other.

Owned for many years by Fleetwood Amusements, the pier was closed at the end of 2000, with the company going into liquidation. The changing of Sunday trading laws and bad weather were blamed for poor financial results. The pier was taken over by Persian Leisure Ltd in 2003, and after a £2 million makeover, was reopened in December that year offering a range of bars, restaurants and entertainment. It is now owned by local Entertainer Mike Simmons who has applied to redevelop the site with flats.

LEFT: An aerial photograph of Fleetwood Pier taken in 1947. Five years later, it was almost completely destroyed by fire. *(English Heritage)*
BELOW: The pier pictured shortly after the addition of the pavilion in 1911. *(Richard Riding collection)*

FOLKESTONE VICTORIA 1888-1954

Plans for a pier at Folkestone were put forward no fewer than three times between 1874 and 1881, and on each occasion they were thwarted by the local town council. Having finally been accepted in the mid-1880s, work on the pier began in March 1887. A compact and elegant structure, the 683ft pier featured a 700-seat pavilion and cost £45,000 to build. On 21 July 1888, the pier was officially opened by Lady Folkestone and named the Victoria Pier to commemorate the Queen's Golden Jubilee. On the first day of opening, 7000 people passed through the turnstiles, boding well for the future of the pier.

A floating landing stage was added to the pier head in 1890, though this was little used. In the same year, new directors were appointed in an effort to make the pier profitable, and in 1903, control of the pier passed to Messrs. Keith Prowse. Under their direction, the landing stage was removed and big names such as Lillie Langtry were engaged to perform at the pavilion. When the Victoria Pier Syndicate took over in 1907, it is claimed that the first international beauty contest was staged on the pier. In addition, a cinema was added and other attractions introduced to the pier.

During the years leading up to World War 2, ownership of the pier changed several times. It remained open for the first few months of the war but was sectioned on 11 June 1940 when the centre span was blown up by the Royal Engineers, leaving the pavilion detached from the shore. In 1943, a makeshift bridge was constructed so that a pipeline could be laid along the length of the pier, enabling seawater to be pumped inland to deal with fires caused by enemy action. After the army moved off the pier in June 1944, the public was allowed back onto the derelict structure. A post-war future looked possible until 20 May 1945 when the pavilion was destroyed by fire and the entire pier badly damaged. Attempts to deal with the fire were hampered by the breach that had yet to be filled. This disaster was the final straw for Folkestone's pier and the cast-iron substructure, reduced to a local eyesore, was finally demolished between 1952 and 1954.

ABOVE: This aerial view of Folkestone Victoria Pier was taken in 1931. *(English Heritage)*
LEFT: Folkestone Pier in 1936 looking east, with the harbour pier, rebuilt in 1904, in the background. *(Richard Riding collection)*
OPPOSITE: An aerial photograph of Folkestone Pier taken in August 1933. *(English Heritage)*

GREAT YARMOUTH BRITANNIA 1901

Today's Britannia Pier is the second to be built on this site, both piers suffering more than their fair share of bad luck. Back in 1857, a 700ft wooden pier was built to receive steamers whilst open-air band performances took place during the summer season. However, in 1859, the pier was cut in half by a drifting ship, repeated in 1868 when the schooner *Sea Gull* crashed through the structure. In 1880, a roof was added to the band area and concerts became a regular feature. At the end of the 1900 season, the first pier was completely demolished and work began on a new structure in December.

The new 810ft pier was built by the Widnes Foundry Company at a cost of £6,000 and featured an unusually large platform at the seaward end. Soon after the pier's opening in June 1902, a domed and turreted 2,000-seat pavilion was completed, built by Norwich-based Boulton & Paul, later to become prolific designers and producers of aircraft. However, the pavilion's life was cut short on 22 December 1909 when it burned down. The replacement suffered a similar fate in April 1914, with suffragettes thought to be responsible. Another pavilion was built in double quick time and opened a few weeks later on 27 July. The floral ballroom was opened in May 1927, but on 3 August 1932, this was also wrecked by fire. It was replaced with the grand ballroom in 1933, the name being changed to the Ocean Ballroom in 1947.

The pier was breached in 1940 as a defence measure but was repaired and reopened for the 1947 season. Prince Little and Tom Arnold had acquired a substantial interest in the pier and top entertainers such as Ken Dodd and Bob Monkhouse were booked for the summer shows. Unbelievably, fire swept through the pier once again on 20 April 1954, and the third pavilion and the Ocean Ballroom were destroyed. The fourth pavilion, the 1,500-seat Britannia Theatre, described as 'better inside than out' in the Pevsner guide, was opened on 27 June 1958; the ballroom was never replaced. After the succession of fires and other setbacks, the last 50 years have been comparatively quiet for the pier. Since 1995, the Britannia Pier has been owned by Family Amusements Ltd, and is one of the few remaining piers to have a working theatre.

ABOVE LEFT: An aerial view of the Britannia Pier taken in August 1938. *(English Heritage)*
LEFT: The pier's pavilion ablaze on 22 December 1909. *(Richard Riding collection)*
FAR LEFT: A postcard view c.1910 showing the helter-skelter that ended up as a house ten miles away at Potter Heigham. *(Richard Riding collection)*
OPPOSITE: An aerial view of the pier taken in 1947. The main buildings seen here were destroyed by fire in 1954. *(English Heritage)*

Opened in October 1853, Great Yarmouth's Wellington Pier is one of the earliest to be built in Britain, although little remains of the original structure. Costing £6,776, the 700ft wooden pier, including a 100ft landing stage, was named in honour of the late Duke of Wellington. In 1900, the same year that the adjacent Britannia Pier opened, the council purchased the Wellington Pier for £1,250. Conscious of the competition, the new owners opted for a complete rebuild with a unique twin-towered pavilion influenced by the International Arts & Crafts style.

Additional pier gardens, complete with bandstand, were created inland of the pier, which opened in July 1903. Perhaps the most distinctive feature of this complex, the famous Winter Gardens, is located just north of the pier. Although erected on the present site in 1904, the gardens were originally located on a four-acre site in Torquay! Inspired by Crystal Palace and designed by Watson & Harvey of Torquay, the glass and iron gardens had opened in June 1881. However, they were not commercially successful and were sold to Great Yarmouth in 1903 for £1,300, a tenth of the original cost. Once re-erected, the gardens became a great success; in 1974, the Department of the Environment listed the building as of outstanding architectural and historical interest.

During the early part of the 20th century the pier played host to a variety of entertainments, such as the 'Vagabond Players' and 'Dud's Dreary Drolleries'. In addition there were huge firework displays, roller skating and more sedate activities such as whist drives and community singing. It was during this period that the Pavilion earned its nickname of the 'cow-shed', owing to its 'rustic' tarred roof and glass-topped internal partition walls, giving the impression of stalls in farm buildings. Visiting artistes could be found hanging fishing lines out of the dressing-room windows and hauling them in during performance intervals.

During World War 2, Great Yarmouth was squarely in the east coast firing line, and the town suffered much damage, the worst year being 1941 when nearly 8,000 bombs were dropped in over 150 air raids. The Wellington Pier was blast-damaged during these raids but not seriously.

In 1971, the piles, girders and beams of the structure at the seaward end were renewed at a cost of £30,000. Unfortunately, the pier's fortunes began to dip and by 1986, things had reached such a pitch that the council recommended demolition rather than investing further funds, a suggestion that brought forth vociferous objections from the public. Plans to site a redundant North Sea oil rig at the end of Wellington Pier as a tourist attraction in the 1980s were turned down by the council as being financially and environmentally impractical. For a period, comedian Jim Davidson took control of the whole pier complex, including the theatre, Winter Gardens and skating rink, despite calling it a 'rubbishy pier'! During 2003, Family Amusements Ltd announced a major facelift for the pier and created a 20,000 sq ft family entertainment area and shops. It was also announced that the theatre with its two towers would be retained, though only the metal framework was left at the time of writing.

ABOVE: An aerial photograph of Great Yarmouth Wellington Pier taken on 21 August 1938. *(English Heritage)*
LEFT: The 1903 pavilion pictured shortly after it was opened. *(Richard Riding collection)*
OPPOSITE: This mid-1950s aerial view of Great Yarmouth shows the promenade and piers. Nearest the camera is Wellington Pier, showing the Winter Gardens to good effect. In the middle is Great Yarmouth Jetty, rebuilt in 1953, and in the background is Britannia Pier, in the middle of reconstruction work after the 1954 fire. *(Richard Riding collection)*

HASTINGS 1872

Built in 1869-1872 and designed by Eugenius Birch, Hastings Pier was opened on Britain's first statutory Bank Holiday: 5 August 1872. The structure consisted of 360 cast-iron columns on screw piles supporting a lattice girder framework and wooden decking. The pier's main feature was the 2,000-seat pavilion at the seaward end and the total cost of the venture was £23,250. More than 24,000 people visited the new pier in the first week. Trippers were able to visit Hastings by steamer when a £2,000 landing stage was added in 1885. In 1913, the shore end of the pier was sold to Hastings Corporation to finance the development of shops and an arcade.

Though the pier received little attention from the enemy during World War 1, the pavilion and the seaward end burned down on 15 July 1917. The pavilion was replaced in 1922, and in 1926, a shoreward end pavilion was built, an Art Deco facade added in the 1930s. Storms in 1938 caused £22,000 of damage and forced the pavilion to close whilst repair work was carried out. As with most south coast piers, Hastings was sectioned for the duration of World War 2 and was used by the armed forces for training purposes. However, the pier did not see much in the way of enemy action and was reopened to the public in 1946.

In 1966, a tridome was built to house the Hastings Embroidery, commissioned to mark the 900th anniversary of the Battle of Hastings and opened by H. M. The Queen. The structure was listed as a building of special and architectural interest by the Department of the Environment in 1976. In 1982, the pier celebrated its 110th birthday and one million visitors were recorded. The following year, the pier was sold for £200,000, but later that year, its new owners had to fork out for repairs of around £100,000 following storm damage. From there on, the pier's fortunes took a downward spiral. Declining visitor numbers and increased maintenance costs resulted in the closure of the pier on safety grounds in October 1999. Since then, several owners have attempted to run the pier profitably, but at the end of 2006, it was closed once again. At the time of writing, the pier's commercial future remains uncertain.

LEFT: An Edwardian postcard view. Note the 'Joy Wheel' near the pier entrance. *(Richard Riding collection)*
ABOVE: An aerial view of the pier taken on 22 July 1958. *(English Heritage)*

TOP: An aerial view of Hastings Pier taken in May 1931. *(English Heritage)*
ABOVE: The disastrous fire that destroyed the 2000-seat pavilion on 15 July 1917. *(Richard Riding collection)*
LEFT: An aerial view of the pier taken in 1931. *(English Heritage)*

HERNE BAY 1899

Since 1832, Herne Bay has had three piers. The first, opened in June 1832, was engineered by Thomas Rhodes and was perhaps the longest and most expensive pier of its time. Owing to shallow water, this timber pier extended to 3,613ft to accommodate steamers, the cost of £50,000 being a huge sum in those days. The pier was intended to form part of the route for passengers travelling to the Continent via Herne Bay and then by stagecoach to Dover to meet ships for the the Channel crossing. Before too long, marine worm and borers took their toll on the woodwork, and after 1839, the wooden piles were replaced with cast-iron. Because of the pier's length, a tramway was laid to take passengers and their luggage to and from the boats. Former hand-propelled wagons were replaced with a sail-powered vehicle called Old Neptune's Car but it had to be propelled by hand in the absence of a favourable wind. This silent motive power sometimes caused accidents.

Following demolition of the iron-framed pier c.1870-1871, the Herne Bay Promenade Pier Company financed a more modest structure, built for pleasure and promenading to the design of Wilkinson & Smith. Only 415ft in length and costing a mere £2,000, the new pier was opened by the Lord Mayor of London in 1873. A pavilion, theatre and lock-up shops were added in 1884. The spectre of

LEFT: The grand pavilion pictured c. 1910. (Richard Riding collection)
BELOW: The pier head and visiting steamer, photographed in September 1959. (English Heritage)

the original full-length pier was not far away, and after 1896, Herne Bay's second pier was rebuilt and extended to regain steamer traffic. The whole of the first section was rebuilt after which a track was laid down to enable a crane to extend the pier to 3,787ft. This track was retained for the use of steamer passengers and was opened in April 1899, running from the restaurant to the pier head. The pier itself was officially opened on 14 September 1899.

In 1909, the pier was sold to the Herne Bay Urban District Council having been administered by its builders, Head Wrightson, after the pier company went into liquidation. In 1910, the pier was extended by the Widnes Foundry Company and a grand pavilion opened near the widened entrance. In 1928, the wooden theatre and frontage shops were destroyed in a fire; the shops were replaced but not the theatre. The pier tramway was discontinued in November 1939 and with the onset of war, the structure was heavily fortified and breached in two places to deter invaders. The East Coast Floods of 1953 caused damage and by the late 1960s, the pier had become unsafe, being closed in 1968. The grand pavilion was destroyed by fire in 1970, and in January 1978, the long neck was damaged by gales leaving the pier head detached from the main structure, a state it remains in today. A sports and leisure complex was opened on the site of the pavilion in September 1978. Herne Bay Pier needs restoring and current estimates are around £12 million. At the time of writing, a charitable trust was being set up.

LEFT: An early aerial view of the pier taken in 1920. *(English Heritage)*
BELOW: Since 1978, the pier head has been isolated from the rest of the structure. *(English Heritage)*

In its day, J. W. Wilson's pier at Hunstanton was regarded as the finest in East Anglia. Rapidly built in 1869-1870, the elegant 830ft pier was officially opened on Easter Day 1870 and was an immediate success; so much so that where entry had initially been free, promenaders were asked to pay 2d or 1d for a child. Within a short while it was discovered that the wooden decking was unsafe and the pier was closed for a year whilst repairs were made.

The original pavilion was replaced with a 'handsome and commodious' pavilion around the turn of the century where Arthur Askey, Elsie and Doris Waters and other big names of the pre-war period entertained. On the evening of 11 June 1939, the pavilion, together with the café and waiting rooms, went up in smoke shortening the pier to 675ft. Though never rebuilt after the war, the space left by the pavilion was used for roller-skating and dancing, weather permitting.

In 1957, the pier attracted a great deal of attention during the production of Ealing Studios' *Barnacle Bill*. It played the part of a pier masquerading as the RMS (Really Motionless Ship) *Arabella* in which the captain, played by Alec Guinness, attempted to beat the licensing laws of the neighbouring resort of 'Sandcastle-on-Sea'. It was one of the last films produced by the studio. During 1958, the pier received a makeover and amusements were added to the arena below the restaurant. At about this time, a pier train was introduced with wooden carriages hauled by a Bassett Lowke steam engine, but this venture was short-lived. In time, the neglected structure became unsafe, and though it survived the Great East Coast Floods of January 1953, it succumbed to a similar catastrophe on 11 January 1978 and was mostly swept away by a storm.

TOP RIGHT: A dramatic view of the fire that destroyed the pavilion and pier head buildings on 11 June 1939. *(Richard Riding collection)*
RIGHT: A rare colour aerial view taken in 1966. The 'Victorian' kiosks visible on the neck were props created in order to embellish the pier for the filming of *Barnacle Bill*. Once completed, the filmmakers agreed to leave them behind! *(English Heritage)*
BELOW: An aerial view of Hunstanton Pier taken in 1920 showing the original pierhead buildings. *(English Heritage)*

Lee-on-Solent, on Southampton Water, was developed as a resort in the late 1800s by Sir J. C. Robinson from Swanage. In 1885, shortly after he acquired the land, an iron pier began to take shape, reportedly on the site of an earlier wooden structure. The 750ft pier, fairly unremarkable in design, cost £10,000 and opened in time for the 1888 season. It featured shelters and a small pavilion where Noel Coward reportedly made his theatrical debut in 1911. During the holiday season, ferries operated to and from Southsea's Clarence Pier.

Following fire damage to the pier in 1932, the foreshore was redeveloped with a large Art Deco building featuring a striking 120ft high white tower, known simply as Lee Tower. The tower had an observation room affording panoramic views of the Solent and the Isle of Wight. Had the planners had their way, the tower would have been over 360ft in height. Described as an ambitious but vulgar piece of architecture, the tower helped put Lee-on-Solent onto the tourist map and attracted visitors to the resort and its pier.

During World War 2, the pier's deck was partially lifted for defence purposes, though later repaired by the US Army and used a launch point for the D-Day landings in June 1944. After the war, a Captain Cutler tried unsuccessfully to operate a ferry service to Cowes using an old RAF rescue launch. The pier was later purchased by Gosport Council who planned to renovate it and recommence steamer services. Nothing came of this and the pier was dismantled in 1958. Lee Tower was demolished in 1971.

LEFT: An aerial photograph of Lee-on-Solent pier taken in 1928, before the redevelopment of the foreshore and building of Lee Tower. *(English Heritage)*
BELOW: The pier pictured in the mid-1920s. The entrance building was the Golden Hall where one could dance, take tea and listen to music. *(Richard Riding collection)*

LLANDUDNO 1877

Along with Bangor Pier further along the north Welsh coast, Llandudno can claim to be one of the least-altered Victorian seaside piers. The first building on the site was a jetty of *c.*1856, but this was cleared to make way for the first phase of the present pier, built in 1876-1877 and initially 1234ft long. Built in two sections, the main pier had a wrought-iron lattice girder framework carried on cast-iron columns extending out to a 60ft wide T-shaped pier head. In 1884, the pier was given a unique 'reverse extension' at the shoreward end, the additional section bypassing the Grand Hotel to link the pier with the promenade. As a result, there are two entrances to the pier and a 45-degree bend where the original and extended parts of the pier meet.

A 2,000-seat, three-storey theatre was built at the pier entrance and officially opened in September 1886. By now, the pier was being extensively used by steamers operating to and from the Isle of Man, and following the enlargement of the pier head, a new landing stage was built in 1891, further reinforced in 1901. In 1905, the seaward end pavilion was built. The pier was often the site for political rallies; Baldwin, Lloyd George, Attlee and Churchill spoke there over the years. Following its acquisition by Trust House Forte in 1968, the landing stage was rebuilt in steel and concrete. The pier's unspoilt Victorian appearance led to it being disguised to represent Blackpool Central Pier for ITV's filming of J. B. Priestley's *Lost Empires* in 1985. In the same year, the pier was featured in a Kit Kat advert with the decking seemingly made of chocolate. More recently, the pier was featured in the 2002 adaptation of *The Forsyte Saga*.

The Grade II listed pier pavilion, closed as a theatre since 1990, was destroyed by a mysterious fire on the evening of 13 February 1994 and was demolished. Other than this, the pier remains relatively unspoiled, and at 2295ft in length, is the longest in Wales and the fifth longest pier in Britain.

ABOVE: An aerial view of this photogenic pier taken in June 1955. *(English Heritage)*
LEFT: An Edwardian postcard view of Llandudno pier taken from where the deck bends 45 degrees on to the main structure. *(Richard Riding collection)*

Lowestoft's 760ft Claremont Pier was built in 1902-1903 for the Coastal Development Company, owners of the piers at Felixstowe and Southwold. Claremont Pier had the advantage of standing in deep water, hence its comparatively short length. During 1912-1913, the T-shaped landing stage and pier head were added. The original piles were replaced with longer lasting greenheart timber. The steamer service was suspended in 1939, and in the following year after the fall of France, the army breached the pier as a defence measure. As the danger of invasion passed, a Czechoslovakian army contingent based in the town, built a temporary bridge across the breached structure and the pier became an army training area.

After the war, there was little enthusiasm to restore the pier, which remained breached until 1950. The council showed no interest in buying it so actor

George Studd bought the pier and undertook necessary repair work; a new reinforced concrete platform and pavilion were built by the end of 1950. The pier has the reputation as being one of the finest locations on the East Anglia coast for sea anglers. Disaster struck in 1962 when a storm wrecked the T-shaped head and destroyed a 40ft section of the pier. Little was done until the 1980s when a major restoration programme was carried out. The pier neck was reopened and the shore end buildings were renovated to offer the usual pier amusements and activities. Sadly, the seaward end of the pier remained unsafe and off-limits.

By the mid-1990s, the pier was rapidly deteriorating, and in 1999, was closed and put up for sale for £2.8 million, having been in the Scott family for 35 years. At the time of writing, Claremont Pier was not open to the public and still up for sale.

BELOW: An aerial photograph of Lowestoft's Claremont Pier taken on 20 May 1928. *(English Heritage)*

LOWESTOFT SOUTH 1846

Like Weymouth Commercial, Lowestoft's South Pier looks more like a modified harbour wall, especially when viewed from the air. Lowestoft Harbour was developed from 1831, and engineer William Cubitt was responsible for two narrow 500ft structures known as the Inner North and Inner South piers. In 1844, a company headed by Sir Martin Peto was formed to further develop the harbour and one of the improvements was the building of the 1320ft long South Pier in 1846. The pier was designed so as to terminate at the harbour entrance.

A reading room built on the pier in 1853-1854 was destroyed by fire in 1885. The pavilion that replaced it, built during 1889-1891, became a favourite subject for postcards until it was badly damaged during World War 2 and later demolished. After the war, the pier was acquired by Associated British Ports (ABP) and leased to the local council. A new pavilion designed by Skipper & Corless was opened on 2 May 1956, by which time a miniature railway ran the length of the pier.

During the mid-1970s, many changes took place. The pavilion was brought up to date and the building at the shoreward end was demolished and replaced by a £220,000 leisure centre. In 1989, the pavilion was pulled down in preparation for building a yacht harbour scheme as part of a plan to incorporate the pier into a new marina. When this was shelved through lack of financial support, Waveney Borough Council carried out a £30,000 refurbishment programme that included the building of a new lifeboat station on the site of the old pavilion. The pier was fully reopened in June 1993.

RIGHT: Taken in April 1950, this aerial view looking south shows the positioning of Lowestoft's piers to good effect. The then derelict and breached Claremont Pier can be seen at the top of the photo. The South, Inner North and Inner South piers can also be seen. *(English Heritage)*

BELOW: An Edwardian postcard view of the South Pier showing the elegant pavilion built in 1891. *(Richard Riding collection)*

Lytham Pier in Lancashire was designed by master pier engineer Eugenius Birch and built in 1864-1865. Extending to 914ft, it was built by R. Laidlaw and opened by Lady Eleanor Cecily Clifton on Easter Monday, 17 April 1865. Gates and tollhouses protected the entrance; other facilities included a waiting room, pier head shelter and gas lighting along the full length of the deck.

The pier failed to prosper, especially after St Anne's Pier, located a short distance away, opened in 1885. Lytham Pier was redesigned in 1892 with the addition of a pavilion halfway along the deck. This was enlarged in 1901 and the pier head bandstand replaced with a floral hall. In October 1903, two Preston Navigation Company barges slipped their moorings and crashed into the pier causing an estimated £1,400 of damage.

During the 1920s, the pavilion was in use as a cinema, but in 1927, was destroyed by fire. From here on, the pier slipped further into decline and by the mid-1930s, it had deteriorated to such a point that it became an embarrassment. By 1938, it was closed to the public except for anglers, and although repairs were made to some of the buildings, the structure was decidedly unsafe. It remained in this sad state until 1960 when, despite protests from local residents, it was demolished in the spring of that year, the council refusing to pay the £5,000 estimated to save it. The cost of demolition was around £7,000, of which £4,000 was paid to the pier owner.

LEFT: The abandoned and dilapidated Lytham Pier photographed in 1955. The level platform in the middle of the pier is where the 1892 pavilion stood; it was destroyed by fire in 1927. (*English Heritage*)
BELOW: The ever-popular donkeys lined up on Lytham sands before World War 1. (*Richard Riding collection*)

MARGATE 1855-1978

Margate's Pier, or Jetty, as it was known, was an important structure for three reasons. It was the first of at least fourteen piers designed by Eugenius Birch, the first to be constructed of iron, and the first pier to have screw piles to secure its legs to the beach. However, Birch's pier was not the first such structure to allow residents and trippers to walk over the sea. As far back as 1808, a pier of sorts had evolved from a pre-existing landing stage at Margate, and had a bandstand and promenade. In 1824, a 1,000ft oak-framed jetty was erected by the Margate Pier Harbour Company and financed by Daniel Jarvis, after whom it was known as Jarvis's Jetty. Though covered by water at high tide, it became a popular venue for promenading at low water. After it was breached in two places during a storm on 4 November 1851, the Harbour Company commissioned Eugenius Birch to design a replacement – his first pier.

The iron structure was built between 1853 and 1857, being opened in a partly completed form in 1855. During 1875-1878, the jetty was lengthened and a hexagonal pier head added, together with a pavilion designed by G. G. Page. In the course of these works, on 24 November 1877, a drifting boat hit the structure and caused £4,000 of damage. People stranded on the pier head could not be rescued until the following day. During World War 2, steamers were suspended whilst the jetty was used by the military for troop and supply movements. After the war, services resumed and continued until their cessation in 1966. By this time, all the pier head buildings had been cleared and the hexagonal platform completely decked over.

By the mid-1970s, the structure was deteriorating and was closed in 1976. The storm of 11 January 1978 dealt a severe blow to British piers. Not only did it destroy Margate Jetty, leaving the lifeboat station isolated and inaccessible, it also destroyed Hunstanton Pier and severely damaged those at Herne Bay and Skegness. Though repeated attempts were made to demolish the remains of the jetty during the late 1970s and early 1980s, Birch's screw piling stubbornly refused to be moved. The pier head's skeletal remains survived until 1998 when they were finally dismantled by the salvage company Eurosalve.

BELOW: This early aerial photograph of the pier was taken in 1920. Note the twin lifeboat slipways. *(English Heritage)*
BELOW LEFT: An Edwardian postcard view of the seaward end of Margate Jetty. *(Richard Riding collection)*
OPPOSITE: This aerial photograph shows a paddle steamer approaching Margate Jetty in 1935. *(English Heritage)*

MINEHEAD 1901-1940

Minehead was comparatively late in acquiring its pier, with the 700ft structure completed in 1901. Designed by J. J. Webster, whose track record included Bangor and Dover piers, Minehead Pier was built of cast-iron and featured a deep-water landing stage just off the pier head. Apart from two tollbooths at the pier's entrance, the structure served primarily as a landing stage for P & A Campbell's popular services to Bristol, Cardiff, Ilfracombe, Lynmouth and elsewhere. A building was erected across the pier neck and a small trolley for carrying luggage ran down the centre of the decking. Other than this, the pier remained comparatively plain in design.

Minehead was one of the few pier casualties of World War 2 and was demolished upon the order of the military during 1940 in order to give nearby gun batteries a clear line of sight. In the mid-1990s, plans were put forward for a new £5 million pier. Sadly however, the Lottery Fund rejected the application.

RIGHT AND BELOW: Two views of the pier taken c.1930. *(English Heritage (right), Richard Riding collection (below))*

The Lancashire resort of Morecambe once boasted two piers; sadly neither exists today. The Morecambe Pier Company was registered in 1867, and on 25 March 1869, the 912ft Central Pier was officially opened having cost £10,000. Built primarily to receive pleasure steamers, the original structure had few amenities. Shortly after the opening of nearby Morecambe West End pleasure pier, this situation changed with the addition of two pavilions in 1897. Both were destroyed by fire on 31 July 1933. A new £25,000, 2,000-seat pavilion/ballroom built in the Art Deco style was opened in 1936.

The pier was partly closed at Easter 1986 after wooden floor decking gave way whilst a disco was being held in the ballroom at the seaward end of the pier. The amusement arcade at the shore end continued in operation until a fire broke out on 4 February 1987. The council served a closure order on the owners, the McAnulty brothers, who then planned to demolish the pier head area.

In 1990, a consortium of businessmen purchased the deteriorating pier, and whilst it was cleared of rubbish, it remained closed. In October 1990, it was offered for sale at £400,000 but there were no takers, especially after another fire destroyed the ballroom on Easter Sunday 1991. At the height of its popularity, 2,000 people would pack the ballroom every night; its floor was praised as one of the finest in the north of England. Sadly, the remains of the pier were demolished during 1992, leaving the seaside resort pier-less.

TOP RIGHT: An aerial photo showing the 2000-seat pavilion that was opened in 1936. *(English Heritage)*
RIGHT: This aerial photo was taken just weeks before the fire of July 1933 that destroyed the pier head pavilions. *(English Heritage)*
BELOW: The interior of the Central Pier's 1936 Marine Ballroom. *(Richard Riding collection)*

MORECAMBE WEST END 1896-1978

Morecambe's second pier was destined to become one of the most ill fated of all pleasure piers. Built in 1895-1897 by the Widnes Iron Foundry and Messrs Mayoh & Haley, the 1800ft structure was officially opened on 3 April 1896, with the pavilion completed the following Easter. The pier was extended in 1898 and the owners purchased its own steamer, *Lady North*, as a popular attraction.

The first of many disasters to plague the pier occurred on 27 February 1903. During a ferocious gale, two large sections of the pier were washed away resulting in the abandonment of any further extension plans. Another gale on 17 March 1907 wrecked the pier again. Sixty yards of the extended section were washed away, as were the toll offices at the pier entrance. The pier head remained isolated out to sea until 1910, by which time the rest of the pier had shrunk to about a third of its original length.

The pavilion had remained unscathed, but on the night of 31 May 1917, it caught fire and was completely destroyed, only a hole in the decking marking its former position. Although some minor buildings were later erected, the pavilion was never replaced. In 1927, another storm relieved the pier of a further 120ft by which time the extended portion of the structure had completely disappeared. The pier was to remain unscathed by the elements for a further fifty years until 11 November 1977 when another storm took its toll and reduced it to a pile of twisted metal at the shore end with the wrecked seaward end marooned out at sea. An eyewitness spoke of the 'horrible groaning and cracking sounds' as the amusement arcade collapsed into the sea. Unable to afford the estimated £5 million required for repair costs, the West End Pier Company had no option but to have the structure demolished in 1978. It is generally agreed that this pier suffered more damage in its lifetime than any other.

BELOW LEFT: Morecambe's West End Pier pictured after it was wrecked by the great storm of 27 February 1903. *(Richard Riding collection)*

BELOW: Taken in 1920, this aerial view shows the largely featureless West End Pier after the 1917 fire. The Central Pier can be seen to the north. *(English Heritage)*

Shortly after the company had completed Morecambe's West End Pier, contractors Mayoh & Hayley and the Widnes Foundry began work on Mumbles Pier on the south Welsh coast. Designed by W. Sutcliffe Marsh, Mumbles' 835ft pier was built on spidery cast-iron legs with steel braces and girders, supporting its wooden decking. A reinforced concrete landing stage was located at the pier head, and halfway down the deck, a thin walkway projected out to the lifeboat station. The pier opened on 10 May 1898 having cost £10,000 to build. It was also the terminus for the Swansea & Mumbles Railway, bringing visitors right to the pier's doorstep until the line's closure in 1960.

In October 1937, the pier was licenced to Amusement Equipment Company Ltd (AMECO) who acquired the freehold in 1957. The pier was breached in 1940 as a defence measure and was extensively rebuilt in the 1950s when a landing jetty was added, the pier reopening on 9 June 1957. Ten years later, a new amusement arcade was built at the entrance. During the intervening years, the owners spent large sums on maintaining and repairing the structure. AMECO continued to own the pier until the expense of maintenance proved too much, forcing closure on 1 October 1987. By this time, the PS *Waverley* had cancelled its visits to the pier due to deterioration of the landing stage.

Following public support, but with little funding, the pier was reopened at Easter 1988 after structural repair work costing £40,000 had been carried out. In 1999, a new pavilion was opened, replacing the old amusement arcade and café, though some decking remained precarious. In the same year, the pier's 10ft fibreglass male gorilla, Nansi, was 'kidnapped' but was returned unharmed and sporting a pair of breasts!

RIGHT: Taken in 1972, this aerial photograph shows the attractive setting of this Welsh pier to good effect. The former railway station can be seen adjacent to the pier's entrance. Note the RNLI lifeboat house and slipway. *(English Heritage)*

British Seaside Piers

NEW BRIGHTON 1867-1977

In 1867, Eugenius Birch designed a 550ft iron pier that replaced the landing stage as used by the New Brighton Ferry. Built by J. E. & A. Dowson, the 660ft pier was opened in September 1867 and completed in April 1868. It featured a central observation tower, saloon, refreshment rooms, shelters and an orchestra. A floating landing stage was linked to the pier via two iron bridges. In 1907, the landing stage became detached from the pier and proceeded to float down the Mersey.

In 1913, a new pavilion was built, and in 1921, the landing stage was renewed. In 1928, the pier was bought by the Wallasey Corporation who spent £31,354 replacing the pier buildings, which had been judged less costly than repairing those existing. World War 2 hardly affected the pier though the structure did provide the base for a searchlight. From the 1960s onwards, the pier fell into decline. In January 1962, the two bridges leading down to the landing stage were badly damaged during a gale, one of them collapsing into the river.

In 1965, the pier was closed because sand accumulating under the pier was preventing steamers from berthing at low tide. It was later leased to Trust House Forte, and after reopening in June 1968, further improvements costing £200,000 were made. However, the problem of silt and sand at the landing stage remained, and by 1971, the number of visitors to the pier had dropped alarmingly. The last boat sailed from New Brighton Pier on 26 September 1971 after which, the pier and ferry were closed and the landing stage towed away to be broken up. In 1977, the pier was demolished.

BELOW: An aerial view taken in 1947. Most of the buildings seen here date from the refurbishment of the late 1920s. *(English Heritage)*

After barrister and hotel owner Arthur Hyde Dendy purchased nearby Teignmouth Pier in 1871, he decided to have it moved to Paignton! When the plan was found to be impractical, a company was formed to build a new pier. Engineered by Gordon Soudon Bridgeman, the 780ft iron pier was opened in June 1879. The pier head boasted an impressive pavilion and a connecting billiards room with two tables. On the death of Dendy, ownership passed to the Devon Dock Pier & Steamship Company, whose paddle steamers became regular visitors from nearby Brixham and Torquay.

On 18 June 1919, a fire swept through the pier head and destroyed the pavilion. From then on, the pier's fortunes took a turn for the worse. The pavilion was not replaced and plans by the local council to purchase the pier for £2,000 in September 1920 came to nothing due to local opposition. Over the next twenty years, the pier neck became the focus for building and commercial development. By 1939, the neck was populated with buildings whilst a miniature racetrack operated on the pier head.

During July 1940, the pier was requisitioned by the War Department and breached as a defence measure, some reports suggesting that all decking was removed. Following repairs after the war, the pier passed to the Cole family. Since then, successive owners have largely succeeded in holding off the ravages of time, with improvement and restoration work being carried out in 1968-1971, 1980-1981 and 1993-1995, the latter carried out by Mitchell Leisure Investments Ltd, owners of Skegness Pier. In its refurbished state, the pier has a less cluttered deck. Very much a 'seaside amusements' pier, it was formally reopened on 7 June 1995 by the Mayor of Torbay, its owners announcing a £1 million 'Back to the Future' project in order to restore the pier to its former Victorian glory.

ABOVE LEFT: This aerial photo was taken in 1953. Note the buildings all the way along the pier neck. *(English Heritage)*
LEFT: A between-the-wars view of the beach area by the pier's entrance. *(Richard Riding collection)*
FAR LEFT: Paignton Pier's pavilion ablaze on 18 June 1919. One hopes that the cast of The Aristocrats as advertised were no longer inside! *(Richard Riding collection)*

PENARTH 1895

Along with Mumbles and Tenby, Penarth was one of three piers built on the south Welsh coast. Taking under two years to build and officially opened on 4 February 1895, it was essentially a 650ft promenade pier with wooden decking on cast-iron piles. In 1907, a wooden pavilion was built at the pier head. During World War 1, the pier was requisitioned, and in 1924, was acquired by Penarth Urban District Council. A large Art Deco pavilion was erected at the shore end during 1927-1928 and a concrete landing stage was added around the same time. For a period, the pavilion was used as a cinema and was later named The Marina before becoming The Commodore.

Disaster struck on August Bank Holiday 1931 when fire broke out in the pier head pavilion, gutting it in a matter of minutes. The blaze also destroyed the shelters and shops in the middle of the pier along with much of the decking. Luckily, the 800 or so people on the pier at the time were shepherded to safety without injury. The pier was restored but the seaward pavilion was not to be rebuilt. In May 1947, gales forced the 7,000-ton vessel *Port Royal Park* to crash broadside into the pier causing £28,000 damage. Repairs were carried out and the pier reopened in 1950. Between 1994 and 1998, restoration work costing over £3 million was carried out, partly funded by the Heritage Lottery Fund. With much of the steelwork and decking renewed, the fully restored pier officially reopened on 14 May 1998.

ABOVE: An Edwardian postcard view of the original entrance to Penarth Pier. *(Richard Riding collection)*
RIGHT: This 1929 aerial view shows the pier at an interesting point in its history, shortly after the opening of the shore end pavilion and new landing stage, but before the pier head pavilion and shelters were destroyed by fire just two years later. *(English Heritage)*

Plymouth Hoe's promenade pier was the idea of local man Ernest Lancaster and was designed by Eugenius Birch. It was to be Birch's fourteenth and final pier as he passed away shortly before Plymouth Hoe was to open. Work on the 420ft pier began in January 1880, though problems with contractors meant it was not completed until four years later. The pier was built over solid rock with 142 piles supporting the wooden decking. It was unusual in that the wide neck area sloped down to the banjo-shaped landing stage, initially consisting of a horseshoe-shaped covered area with a post office, reading room and refreshment rooms. The pier head's centre was left empty whilst staircases led down to embarkation points for steamers. The pier was opened on 29 May 1884 and cost £45,000 to build.

In 1887, Walter Kay, a local fish merchant, purchased the pier for £12,000. In 1891, a 2,000-seat pavilion was built on the pier head. In addition to serving as a dance and concert hall, boxing matches, concert parties and roller-skating were also staged there. Steamers docked at the pier until 1922 when the pier company sold its fleet, after which its fortunes began to slide, culminating in receivership in 1938. On 21 March 1941, the pier was badly damaged during a particularly heavy night bombing raid, leaving the pavilion a twisted shell. With shades of Brighton West, the pier was left derelict for many years until it was removed in 1953, the War Damage Commission meeting the cost of £4,754.

BELOW: An aerial photograph of the pier taken in 1937. *(English Heritage)*

RAMSEY QUEEN'S 1886

Built primarily for the use of steamers, Queen's Pier at Ramsey on the Isle of Man was designed by Sir John Coode and constructed by Head Wrightson of Stockton on Tees. Work began on the 2248ft structure in June 1882 and it was officially opened on 22 July 1886. During the first year, 159 steamers landed at the pier, most of them from Belfast, Fleetwood and Liverpool. As with Herne Bay, a 3ft gauge trackway initially laid to transport materials was adapted as a baggage tramway. At first, the stock was horse-drawn but from 1937, a small petrol-driven Hibberd Planet engine replaced them.

On 25 August 1902, King Edward VII and Queen Alexandra landed at the pier; other Royal visitors included King George V and Queen Mary on 14 July 1920. They were just some of the average 36,000 passengers that annually used the pier during the period. In 1970, the pier was closed to ferry passengers, and in 1981, the tramway was closed and the lines lifted. In July 1982, work began to demolish the unsafe and redundant east berth and the pier was closed to the public on 22 April 1991 following outbreaks of vandalism and continued deterioration. The south landing stage was later demolished.

A petition demanding that the pier be restored and put back into use had no effect but eventually, in December 1993, a working party set up by the Manx government submitted a report examining the options for its demolition or restoration. Estimates for demolition amounted to more than £1 million whilst those for restoring the structure were more than £2.5 million. In January 1994, the Friends of The Queen's Pier was set up to restore the pier to its original form and reopening to the public. During 1996, some essential repair work took place and a consultant's report in 1999 judged the structure to be in sound condition. Despite this however, the pier remains closed and its future is uncertain.

ABOVE: Queen's Pier Ramsey c.1905. Because Queen's was built primarily as a low water landing pier for steamers, there was little in the way of pleasure or entertainment facilities. *(Richard Riding collection)*
LEFT: An aerial view of the pier taken in June 1959. Carried on 60 spans, the average width of the pier is 20 feet. *(English Heritage)*

Redcar Pier was one of six piers built between the Humber and Tees estuaries, and all suffered as a result of their exposed position on the northeast coast. The notion of a pier at Redcar was mooted as far back as 1866 but the idea went cold until neighbouring Coatham expressed interest in a pier. Rather than build a single pier for the two resorts, each went their own way; Coatham's pier was opened in 1873 whilst work on Redcar began in the summer of 1871.

Designed by J. E. & A. Dowson of London, the pier was built by Head Wrightson & Company of Stockton. The 1300ft long pier was opened on 2 June 1873 and featured a bandstand, three kiosks at the entrance, a landing stage and a 700-seat bandstand on the pier head. The pier received more than its fair share of misfortunes over the next 25 years, the first occurring in October 1880 when the brig *Luna* was driven through the pier by a severe storm. On 1 January 1885, the S.S. *Cochrane* demolished the landing stage. The pier company was unable to make repairs and steamers bypassed the resort in favour of Redcar's neighbours. Then, on 12 January 1897, wreckage from the Norwegian schooner *Amarant* caused a 60ft breach in the pier. To cap it all, on 20 August 1898, the pier head and the bandstand burned down. Perhaps the only consolation was that soon after, Coatham Pier was destroyed, thus removing Redcar Pier's closest competition.

The early 20th century saw an improvement in fortunes, with a pavilion and ballroom built at the shore end in 1909 and extended in 1928. However, after the pier was breached in 1940, a drifting mine caused extensive damage exacerbated by succeeding storms. By 1946, only the pavilion and some 45ft of the neck remained. After the Redcar Pier Company was wound up in 1946, the local borough council purchased what was left of the pier with the intention of restoring it. Soon after this work was carried out, the devastating East Coast storms of January 1953 caused further damage to the pavilion and its supporting structure. By 1980, the pier was decidedly unsafe and was closed. Upon receiving an offer to buy and dismantle the pier for just £250, the council agreed and demolition took place in 1981.

ABOVE: An Edwardian postcard view shows the pier in its original form, with just three minaret kiosks at the entrance. *(Richard Riding collection)*
LEFT: An aerial view of the pier taken in 1924, showing the 1907 pavilion. *(English Heritage)*

RHOS-ON-SEA / DOUGLAS 1869-1954

To date the most interesting aspect about the pier at Rhos-on-Sea is the fact that it formerly stood at Douglas on the Isle of Man. Douglas Pier was designed by London engineer John Dixon and opened in August 1869, having taken just five months to build. A commercial failure, it was sold in 1894 with Dixon brought back in to oversee its re-erection, in slightly longer form, at Rhos-on-Sea the following year. Fortunately, the pier had been designed in such a way that it could be dismantled almost as easily as it was originally erected.

Rhos Pier faced stiff competition from the nearby piers at Llandudno and Colwyn Bay and never prospered. As can be seen from the aerial photo, it was a promenade pier with little on the superstructure other than a pair of shelters at the seaward end. With the outbreak of war in 1939, the wooden pier decking was breached, although the iron framework was left in place. Several drifting mines narrowly missed the pier, yet despite this apparent good fortune, it never reopened after 1945 and was finally demolished in 1954. The stone-built toll room still remains today on Rhos Point and houses a souvenir shop and small museum.

LEFT: A pre-World War 1 picture of the pier after it was moved to Rhos-on-Sea from Douglas, Isle of Man. *(Richard Riding collection)*
BELOW: This rare aerial photograph of Rhos-on-Sea Pier was taken in 1920. *(English Heritage)*

Rhyl Pier was the second of four piers designed by James Brunlees and the longest seaside pier in Wales. The 2355ft structure cost £15,000 to build, and after opening in 1867, was used primarily by steamers sailing between Liverpool and Welsh resorts. Throughout its lifetime, Rhyl Pier was to fall victim to the weather and collisions. In December 1883, the schooner *Lady Stuart* hit the pier and demolished 180ft of the structure, and in 1891, the *Fawn* caused further damage. That same year, the Grand Pavilion was opened at the entrance, whilst the smaller Bijou Pavilion was erected at the seaward end. Attractions included diving competitions and, according to one handbill, 'Walking the Greasy Pole'!

The Grand Pavilion was destroyed by fire in 1901 and storms resulted in the collapse of one section of the pier. With the constant battering by the elements, the pier was declared unsafe in 1913 and was closed to the public. After festering for several years, the pier was acquired by the local council in the 1920s. The shore end was developed with the addition of the red brick amphitheatre; however, the seaward end was demolished. The pier reopened in 1930 and remained in business for another 36 years, although another short section was demolished around 1945, reducing its length to a mere 330ft. Once again, safety concerns were raised and the pier was closed for good in 1966. It was finally put out of its misery and dismantled in March 1973.

LEFT: This aerial photograph taken in 1947 shows the unusual curving path of the pier neck. *(English Heritage)*
BELOW: An aerial view of Rhyl Pier in 1966, the year it was closed. *(English Heritage)*

One of the most frequently asked questions concerning British piers is, 'When was the first pleasure pier built?' Ryde Pier on the Isle of Wight is generally regarded as the first and its inception dates back to 1812, when John Kent of Southampton designed the structure. Because of the mudflats around the Ryde foreshore, it was necessary for the wooden pier to extend out to deeper water to facilitate the berthing of sailing vessels. The 1714ft pier took a year to build and opened on 26 July 1814 having cost £16,000.

The completed structure was only 12ft in width and was essentially a very long jetty, making it vulnerable to weather and collisions. Initially there was no landing stage, just a flight of steps leading down to the water. With the advent of steamships, the pier was extended to 2024ft in 1824, and in 1827, the pier head was enlarged to accommodate two steamers at a time. In 1833, the structure was extended to its ultimate length of 2250ft: nearly half a mile. In February 1838, a storm blew a brig into the pier and 50ft of the structure was badly damaged with the brig sinking. The pier head was further enlarged and rebuilt at a cost of £400 and between 1856-1860, it was further lengthened whilst the small pavilion was moved to the western side and used as a refreshment kiosk.

By the 1860s, Ryde was becoming a very popular resort, being described as the 'Gateway to the Island', with many visitors arriving by boat. To cope with the increased traffic, a second pier was built alongside the existing structure equipped with a horse-drawn tramway. In February 1872, gas lighting was installed at the end of the pier, and in 1877, work started on a third pier adjacent to the tramway to carry a railway to the pier head. This was opened on 12 July 1880. From 1895, the pier's wooden piles were replaced with those of iron. Working from the seabed, the task was completed by 1911.

A pavilion was built on the pier head in the same year, supported on iron piles and reinforced concrete below the water line. The domed two-storey building could seat more than 700 people. During 1917, a twice-daily steamer service was introduced between Portsmouth and Ryde. In March 1918, a storm wrecked 750ft of the pier but the damage was repaired. By 1922, the lifeboat station had closed, and in June 1924, the Southern Railway took over the pier. During the early 1930s, the wooden pier head was rebuilt in concrete. The tramway pier closed in 1969, the pavilion demolished in 1971 and a five-year re-planking programme began. The railway was electrified in 1967 and the line still uses ex-London Underground tube stock, though only one platform remains at the pier head railway station. Although Ryde Pier was designated a listed building in 1976 it had changed dramatically, and since then most of the pier head platform has been cleared and converted to car parking.

LEFT: This aerial photograph taken in June 1961 shows the fully extended Ryde Pier. *(English Heritage)*
OPPOSITE: An aerial view of Ryde pier head taken in August 1939. *(English Heritage)*

British Seaside Piers

ST ANNE'S 1885

Some 20 years after Lytham Pier was opened in 1865, another pier, opposite the Ribble Estuary, was officially opened at St Anne's, some 3.5 miles away as the seagull flies. Work began in 1879, and although the 914ft structure was comparatively plain, it took six years to complete, being finally opened by Fred (later Lord) Stanley on 15 June 1885. Around 1900, a mock-Tudor entrance building was erected which still stands today.

In April 1904, the pier was embellished with the addition of the 1000-seat Moorish Pavilion on the wide pier head platform, along with several kiosks and other improvements. To the other side of the pier head, the Floral Hall was opened in June 1910, which attracted many famous performers including Gracie Fields and George Formby. By now the pier was attracting many visitors, as well as steamers from Blackpool and Liverpool, calling at the L-shaped landing jetty. In 1922, St Anne's and nearby Lytham were formally amalgamated to become Lytham St Anne's and for over 15 years, the town had two active piers. Lytham's pier closed in 1938 and was demolished in 1960. In 1954, an amusement arcade was built by the entrance of St Anne's Pier; re-decking was carried out in the late 1950s and a restaurant built. After 1962, new owners carried out further improvement work to the jetty, entrance buildings and Floral Hall.

St Anne's Pier gradually lost the steamer trade after the Ribble Navigation Act of 1883 later resulted in the dredging of channels to enable large vessels to access Preston. As a consequence of the dredging, sand built up and the pier was left high and dry, inaccessible to steamers. Two fires brought about the end of St Anne's Pier as it had stood since the Edwardian times. In 1974,

ABOVE: Edwardians paddling near the pier at the turn of the 20th century. *(Richard Riding collection)*
RIGHT: This aerial photograph was taken in July 1920 and shows the Moorish Pavilion and Floral Hall adjacent to each other at the seaward end. *(English Heritage)*

the famous Moorish Pavilion was destroyed and the owners forced into liquidation. Though threatened with partial demolition, its new owners sought to repair the structure, but a second fire in July 1982 destroyed the Floral Hall and necessitated the demolition of the entire seaward end, reducing the pier's length to 600ft. Repairs to the shore end buildings, now the focus of the pier's attractions, were carried out in the 1990s.

A shadow of its former self, St Anne's Pier is well regarded for its fine wrought iron work and range of facilities. In 2002, plans were announced for a new hi-tech all-weather pier with a 200ft high tower, to be designed by Mark Seddon.

TOP: Overdressed Edwardians on the beach at St Anne's before World War 1.
ABOVE: Opened around 1900, the pier's mock-Tudor entrance building still stands today. *(Both: Richard Riding collection)*
LEFT: An aerial view of St Anne's Pier in 1971. The entire pier head platform has since disappeared. *(English Heritage)*

ST LEONARDS PALACE 1891-1951

St Leonards Palace was the first of four piers designed by London engineer Richard St George Moore (1858-1926). Construction of the 960ft pier was put in the hands of Head Wrightson and work began in 1888. It was officially opened by Lord and Lady Brassey on 28 October 1891 and cost £30,000 to build. It featured a 700-seat pavilion with a dance hall and refreshment rooms built near the shore end.

Although the pier was equipped with a landing stage, there was little in the way of steamer activity, and after it was destroyed by gales, it was not replaced. The pier prospered until the resident orchestra moved elsewhere, after which its fortunes went into decline, not helped by the proximity of neighbouring Hastings Pier. In the 1930s, the pier was purchased by the Lannon brothers who, in an effort to stem the fall in patronage, introduced some interesting but controversial changes. At about this time, the pier entrance was revamped and given an Art Deco style frontage.

In common with most south coast piers, St Leonards was breached as a defence measure during World War 2. It also suffered bomb damage during an air raid on 4 October 1940 and was further damaged by fire. The once elegant pier remained closed after the war and suffered further damage following a severe gale on 13 March 1951. This final blow gave Hastings Corporation no alternative but to have the structure demolished the same year.

ABOVE: An Edwardian view of St Leonards Palace pier. *(Richard Riding collection)*
TOP RIGHT: This 1933 low-level aerial photograph shows the more functional pier head pavilion, then in use as a skating rink. Note the complexity of the substructure. *(English Heritage)*
RIGHT: A 1935 aerial view showing the shoreward end of the pier. *(English Heritage)*

Saltburn is the last surviving of six Victorian piers built along the East Yorkshire coast. Tide and winds have taken their toll of the other five. After the formation of the Saltburn Pier Company in 1867, local man John Anderson was appointed both engineer and contractor and the 1500ft structure was officially opened in May 1869. Some 20ft wide, the pier featured a saloon and landing stage at the pier head, octagonal kiosks at its entrance and refreshment booths in the centre.

The pier attracted steamers from nearby Whitby and Scarborough, and for the first four years, the venture was a financial success. However, in October 1875, the all-important landing stage was wrecked in a storm and the pier was not reopened until 1877, minus 250ft at the sea end. Following liquidation of the owners, the Saltburn Improvement Company acquired it in 1879. During the 1880s, a bandstand was added, electric illuminations installed and the entrance kiosks were replaced with larger buildings. In 1884, an inclined tramway replaced a vertical hoist on the cliff opposite the pier's entrance.

During 7-8 May 1924, the vessel *Ovenbeg* smashed into the structure causing a 210ft gap, isolating the pier head bandstand until repairs were made in 1930. In 1939, the pier was breached again, this time by the army, as an invasion precaution. During the 1950s, the pier was only open from time to time. Though fully repaired in 1947, its reopening in 1952 was short-lived after gales the following year prompted yet another closure until 1958. Once the pier had passed its centenary it was beginning to show its age; rusting of the metalwork, coupled with dodgy steel piling saw the Grade II listed structure closed at the end of 1973. When the local council announced its intention to demolish the pier, local feelings ran high and a public enquiry resulted in a two-year restoration programme. The refurbished pier, reduced to 681ft long, was reopened on 29 June 1978. During 2000-2001, further reconstruction work was carried out. With Heritage Lottery funding, decorative under-deck lighting was installed in 2005.

TOP LEFT: An aerial view of the pier taken in July 1932 after repairs were made to plug the 210ft gap made by the *Ovenbeg* in May 1924. *(English Heritage)*
LEFT: This Edwardian postcard view from the pier shows the inclined tramway scaling the cliff in the background. *(Richard Riding collection)*

SANDOWN CULVER 1879

Although the Sandown Pier Company was formed in the early 1860s, problems with finding the necessary capital meant it was not until 1876 that work started on a 360ft pier. Built by Messrs Jukes & Coulson of London, the pier stood on cast-iron piles and had an iron girder framework with timber decking. It had a small shelter at its head and two tollbooths at the entrance. The pier was opened in time for the 1879 season. By 1887, ownership had passed to the Sandown Pier Extension Company Ltd which, as the name suggested, financed the pier's extension to 875ft in 1895. In the same year, a £12,000 400-seat pavilion was built and a triple berth landing stage erected to enable steamers to call at any time. The opening of the updated pier and its new pavilion took place on 17 September 1895.

The pier was closed during World War 1, and in September 1918, ownership passed to Sandown Urban District Council. Taking only five months to build, the new 1,000-seat shore end pavilion was opened on 23 October 1934 by Admiral of the Fleet Lord Jellicoe. Meanwhile, the smaller pier head pavilion became a ballroom. The pier was breached for the duration of World War 2 during which time the landing stage deteriorated. It was eventually replaced with a concrete double deck structure, which was opened in 1954. The breach was similarly plugged in concrete.

In 1956, during a tour of the island, the Queen and the Duke of Edinburgh arrived at the pier in the Royal Barge and attended a ceremony held in the pavilion. By the mid-1960s, the pier was beginning to show its age and the local council went ahead with a complete rebuild of the structure. Whilst the work was carried out the pier was closed to visitors. The old pavilion was demolished and the landing stage altered to its current distinctive 'hook' shape. With its amusements now updated to suit 20th century tastes, Earl Mountbatten officially reopened the pier on 22 July 1973.

In 1986, the South Wight Borough Council sold the pier to Sandown Pier Ltd, run by businessman George Peak who already had 20 years of experience running the amusement arcade. The pier's theatre was leased back by the council and during the winter of 1988, a £500,000 refurbishment programme was carried out. Isle of Wight (Theatres) Ltd undertook the running of the theatre, but during the 1989 August Bank Holiday, a fire broke out in the amusement arcade badly damaging the pavilion and adjacent decking. That year's summer show, *Summer Magic*, starring Jimmy Tarbuck, was transferred to the nearby Shanklin Theatre.

Although the shoreward end of the pier was opened less than two days after the blaze, the rest of the structure, including the theatre, underwent a £2 million repair and facelift, reopening in June 1990. In 1997, the restored theatre was closed and later converted into an indoor bowling and golf centre. At the time of writing, George Peak's son, George Wayne Peak, manages Sandown Pier Leisure Ltd.

RIGHT: This aerial view showing the *MV Vecta* at Sandown Pier's three-berth landing stage was taken on 20 August 1939. *(English Heritage)*

Seaview was the longest surviving of three chain piers built in the British Isles, the others being Brighton Chain (1823-1896) and Leith Trinity Chain (1821-1898). Seaview Chain Pier was built to attract steamer traffic to the area and was designed by local man Frank Caws, who went on to oversee its construction by local labourers including sailors and riggers. The pier was opened in June 1881 and consisted of five spans between twin-towered supports, all built with 'Kynaised' (treated) timber. The deck spans had a slight arch to them and their 'switchback' quality was noted in contemporary guidebooks. At first, there was a small pavilion at the pier head and a couple of entrance buildings. The pier head was rebuilt on a larger scale in 1889 and again in 1901, bringing the pier to its final length of 1050ft. Slot machines were introduced with electric lighting following in 1904-1905.

During World War 1, steamer services were suspended as vessels were pressed into war use. Sadly they failed to return to Seaview after the end of hostilities, though steam launches known as 'V' boats continued to bring trippers to the pier. During World War 2, the pier was taken over by the Admiralty, but instead of being breached, it was used to prepare for the D-Day invasion of Normandy. By 1947, the pier was in poor condition and was sold to builder A. J. Figgins for a mere £775. The new owner intended to fully restore the pier, but having been defeated by red tape, he announced his intention to have the ancient structure demolished, much to the displeasure of the locals. The £6,000 estimate for restoration prompted ideas for building a completely new pier. However, Figgins sold the pier to the Horwich brothers, owners of the Pier Hotel, for £1,000. In 1950, Seaview became the country's first pier to be listed but was overwhelmed by a series of storms in December the following year. The storms left little more than the pier head and 100ft of decking remaining and demolition followed in 1952.

TOP LEFT: An aerial view of the decaying pier taken in 1947 – four years later it was destroyed by a series of storms. *(English Heritage)*
LEFT: An Edwardian view of Seaview Chain Pier. *(Richard Riding collection)*

SHANKLIN 1890-1993

Local businessmen formed the Shanklin Esplanade & Pier Company in the early 1870s, but more than ten years would elapse before work on the 1200ft pier began. Designed by F. C. Dixon and M. N. Ridley, the pier was built by John Dixon and Alfred Thorne of London, who began work in August 1888. The pier consisted of an iron girder framework supported on cast-iron piles and had attractive pagoda-style tollbooths at the entrance. The pier was gas lit and supplied with mains water.

On 18 August 1890, Shanklin Pier was opened to steamer services, but receivers were called in, as there were insufficient funds to pay the £24,000 cost of its construction. Though for sale, the pier attracted no buyers and was acquired by Shanklin Urban District Council in 1899. By this time, a small pavilion had been added and the original contractors returned ten years later to build the short-lived Grand Pavilion at a cost of £4,000. Opened on 28 July 1909, the pavilion was destroyed by fire on 29 June 1918. The original 150ft long landing stage was damaged beyond repair and was dismantled.

After Horace Terry Wood purchased the pier in 1925, the pavilion was rebuilt and reopened on 4 June 1927, with a new landing stage constructed in 1931. In 1933, the small pavilion at the pier head was rebuilt with a maple floor and became a very popular dancing venue. Another attraction was Professor Montague Wesley, the one-legged diver, whose speciality was diving off a high platform in flames, wearing a black rubber suit with the missing leg laced up! During World War 2, Royal Engineers blew up the second and third spans of the pier as a defence measure, but the structure was to play a minor part in the war.

ABOVE: Edwardian visitors strolling on Shanklin Pier c.1904. *(Richard Riding collection)*
RIGHT: This aerial view of the pier was taken on 14 April 1977, not long after Fred Sage reopened it. *(English Heritage)*

In order to supply fuel for the Allies during the Normandy landings, a pipeline (PLUTO – Pipe Line Under The Ocean) was laid from the mainland, via Southampton across the Solent to pumping stations on the island: one at Sandown, the other at Shanklin. From Shanklin, the pipeline ran along the pier to the landing stage, though in the event, it was never used.

Still managed by the Terry Wood family, the pier was reopened in 1947 and various improvements were carried out. After the pier was sold in 1970, no fewer than four owners tried to make a go of running it, but receivers were eventually called in and the pier was closed throughout 1975. It reopened in May 1976 under the ownership of Fred Sage who became one of the founders of the National Piers Society. His small team worked hard and succeeded in putting the pier on its feet once more. His secretary even stood in as the pier's disc jockey, earning the name 'The Disco Granny' as a result!

By the early 1980s, repairs were required and the Shanklin Pier Preservation Society was set up to raise the necessary funds. By 1986, the pier was on a sound footing and passed to Leading Leisure plc, who planned to invest £7 million into further development of the pier, including a leisure and conference complex. However, before this could take place a hurricane-force gale (aka The Great Storm) devastated the pier on the morning of 16 October 1987, leaving it broken in three sections (see photos in Introduction).

Plans to repair the pier were delayed and the structure became a local eyesore. After Leading Leisure went bankrupt the receiver tried unsuccessfully to sell the pier. Finally, in February 1993, three years after the pier's 100th birthday, South Wight Borough Council purchased it for £25,000, spending a further £189,000 to have the pier demolished by local company Graham Attrill. Unusually for the time, much of the material was recycled.

BELOW: A low-level aerial view of Shanklin Pier taken in August 1939, showing PS *Princess Elizabeth* berthed at the landing stage. *(English Heritage)*

Strictly speaking Sheerness Pier has no place in this book. Situated away from the town and beach, it was built as a landing stage for boats and provided a vital link between the Isle of Sheppey and the mainland. However, visitors were required to pay a toll for the privilege, which in the view of the authors justifies its inclusion here.

Few details have been unearthed concerning the architects and engineers involved. What is known is that a wooden pier was completed at a cost of £4,400 and opened in September 1835. Steamboat excursions operated to resorts on the Essex and Kent coasts and as far north as East Anglia, for which normal facilities were provided on the pier. Business began to decline after the railway reached the town in 1860, and in November 1897, the pier fell victim to a severe storm during which the wooden piles were drawn like teeth from the seabed. The pier was rebuilt with iron piles and reopened in 1899. This 'new' pier featured a baggage rail line, which ran down the left side of the deck to the pier head. A tearoom was available for promenaders and visitors arriving by steamer, though such excursions were greatly reduced. During the 1920s, the structure was consolidated with the addition of a stone jetty at the shore-end.

The pier was spared breaching during World War 2 but was requisitioned by the Royal Navy and saw much activity when troops landed there at the height of the Dunkirk evacuation. Having survived the war unscathed, the pier was badly damaged when a tugboat sliced through it in 1946 and though later repaired, it was closed by the Admiralty for safety reasons in 1955. Plans to restore the ailing pier came to nothing and it was demolished in 1971 when the Medway Ports Authority acquired it.

BELOW: Taken in August 1947, though appearing like a wartime breach, the damage visible from this aerial view was caused by a drifting tugboat the year before. *(English Heritage)*

The Earl of Scarbrough, who had brought the railway to Skegness in 1873, formed the Skegness Pier Company in 1877 and the design of the pier was advertised as a competition with a prize of £50 for the winner. More than 40 entries were received and engineers Clarke & Pickwell won the competition. Work on the 1817ft structure began in 1880 and the official opening took place on 4 June 1881. The cast-iron pier supported a Jarrah-wood deck upon which was built a 700-seat saloon/concert hall at the T-shaped pier head.

The pier head was extended in 1898 and refreshment rooms were built nearby. In March 1919, the schooner *Europa* breached the pier, and although a temporary gangway bridged the breach, the gap was not properly plugged until 20 years later. In 1937, the Victorian Gothic entrance building was replaced with contemporary styled north and south beach entrances.

During World War 2, the pier was breached and although it survived, its condition was so poor that restoration work costing £23,000 had to be carried out before it reopened to the public in 1948. Five years later the pier suffered damage during the infamous East Coast Floods of January 1953, the £3,000 bill for the repair work being footed by Lord Scarbrough. More changes took place in the early 1970s when the pier entrance buildings were demolished to make way for a new building housing a café, shops and amusements.

The pier received a near-terminal blow on 11 January 1978 when a combination of high tides and a gale washed away two sections of the pier, leaving the pier head and theatre detached from the shore end. Various schemes to restore or develop the structure failed to materialise. Despite becoming Grade II listed in 1984, the marooned section of the structure was demolished, during which time the theatre burned down. Owners Mitchell Leisure have developed the shore end and plan to restore the pier to its former glory.

ABOVE: The pier's second entrance building, opened in 1937. *(Richard Riding collection)*
LEFT: Skegness Pier pictured from the air in 1948, shortly after major restoration work had been carried out. *(English Heritage)*

SOUTHAMPTON 1833-1980

On 8 July 1833, Princess Victoria (later Queen) and the Duchess of Kent officially opened Southampton's 900ft Royal Pier, situated to the west of Town Quay near the Eastern Docks. Its unusual design featured a large pier head platform with two long landing stages extending out at angles. In 1871, rail lines were extended to the pier head and a station was built on a pontoon that had been added in 1864. Steamers to the Channel Islands, Le Havre and the Isle of Wight used the pier.

Reconstruction took place in 1892, and in 1894, a new pavilion provided concerts, dramas and dancing; roller-skating was introduced in 1906. Shortly before World War 1, the pier and the adjacent station had deteriorated and repairs were made. However, the trains did not run during the war and they were not reinstated afterwards. An impressive gatehouse building was built at the entrance in 1930. During the 1950s and 1960s, the 1931 world speed record-breaking Supermarine S.6A seaplane was displayed on the pier.

In January 1980, the 146-year-old pier was closed by the British Transport Docks Board. There was local opposition to this decision, but despite the setting up of the Royal Pier Preservation Society in 1981, the pier remained closed. The 1930 gatehouse was converted into an upmarket pub/restaurant complex, which was later taken over by Leading Leisure plc, owners of Shanklin Pier. The premises were opened in February 1986 and renamed... *The Pier*. Red Funnel took over the shoreward end of the pier in January 1984 for use as a car park. On 4 May 1987, a fire destroyed the ballroom and in 1992, the pier was described as unsafe and beyond economic repair. Today its remains are something of an eyesore and doubtless will be redeveloped in the future, one idea being to build a casino on the site.

LEFT: An aerial photograph taken in 1949 showing the layout of the pier to good effect. *(English Heritage)*
ABOVE: Southampton Royal Pier's pavilion and bandstand *c.*1912. *(Richard Riding collection)*

'The pier is Southend, Southend is the pier,' so said the late Poet Laureate, Sir John Betjeman, who incidentally, was the first President of the National Piers Society on its formation in 1979. Apart from its pier, Southend is also famous for its mud. It was partly because of this that a landing jetty first appeared at Southend as early as 1802, erected by Sir Thomas Wilson, in order to allow Royal Hotel visitors arriving by boat to avoid the mire.

With the inauguration of Southend's first steamship service in 1819, it was soon realised that a longer jetty or pier was required for more general use. To this end, the Southend Pier Company was formed by a private syndicate and in 1829, the first pile was driven for what was to become Britain's third and the world's longest seaside pier. The foundation stone was laid by the then Lord Mayor of London, Sir William Thompson, on 25 July. By May the following year, the first 600ft section of the pier had been completed with piles of oak and was opened in June 1830. Horse-drawn trucks were used to carry passengers and their luggage and in 1875, rails were laid to assist the horses. It was later discovered that the horses' hooves were damaging the wooden decking and the

animals were fitted with special rubber shoes. Initially there were no buildings or entertainments on the pier apart from the 'Octagon', a marquee in which concerts were held. It was hardly the ideal venue as horses had to pass through it!

During 1834-1835, the pier head was further extended and an upper platform was added for receiving steamer passengers; a lower deck was provided for landing goods. Meanwhile, the pier was still far too short to receive steamers other than at high tide, and its wooden structure was fast deteriorating. In 1844, the pier was sold for £17,000 to the Chairman of Eastern Counties Railway. During 1844-1846, the pier was extended to a mile and a quarter, and in 1873, the Local Board purchased it for £12,000, less than the 1844 sale price.

In March 1887, an Act of Parliament authorised the reconstruction of the 'old' pier in steel. James Brunlees and J.W. Barry were appointed designers and work began alongside the old structure in 1888. Construction was entrusted to Arrol Bros. of Glasgow and the pier was officially opened on 24 August 1890. The only part of the old pier to remain was the 1885 brick tollhouse. A new electric single-track railway ran the full length of the pier along its eastern side - the first electric tram service on a pier in the country. A pier extension was built in 1898 at a cost of £22,000 in order to provide greater safety for steamer passengers - 250,000 trippers had landed or embarked the previous season. Between 1901-5 the pier featured a water-chute and during 1907 work began on an upper promenade deck, reached by four stairways on a new extension. Opened by Southend's Mayor on 25 July 1908, it included a new pier head with accommodation for 6000 people, a bandstand and covered seats that extended round the entire deck.

Because of its great length at 7080ft, Southend was particularly susceptible to collisions from ships and also had its fair share of fires. In December 1898, a ketch sliced through the pier and caused more than £1,000 of damage. A hay-laden barge badly damaged the pier in December 1907, and on 23 November 1908, the vessel *Marlborough* cut clean through the pier and destroyed a section that had been completed only months earlier. On 12 July 1909, the barge *Alzima* collided with the pier, and on 4 December 1913, the barge *Basildon* caused further damage. Another serious breach occurred in January 1921 when the concrete motor ship *Violette* caused a 180ft breach in the structure and sank.

The pier remained open throughout World War 1 and played little part in the war effort; it was to be a different story 20 years later. During the interwar years, a second rail track was laid and the Prince George steamer extension was added in 1929. With the outbreak of war in September 1939, Southend and its pier became strategically important and the most heavily defended area in Essex. The pier was taken over by the Royal Navy and became known as *HMS Leigh*, though all three services occupied it in some form or another.

BELOW: An aerial photograph of the shore end of Southend Pier taken in 1950. *(English Heritage)*

The army built an upper deck on the Prince George extension, mounting anti-aircraft guns in concrete emplacements and building pillboxes beyond the pavilion. During World War 2, 3,367 convoys comprising 84,297 vessels sailed out of Southend. The writer A. P. Herbert, who served as a petty officer on *HMS Leigh*, famously said that Southend Pier should have been awarded the George Medal for its wartime service.

The pier had a few close shaves during the war, none closer than a V-2 rocket that fell just to the west of the pier in October 1944. Although it failed to explode, the missile's engine passed through the piers' pavilion into the mud below. Throughout the war, the pier train covered 300,000 miles and carried 1.5 million servicemen and women. The pier was reopened to the public on 27 March 1945 as the war in Europe was coming to a close. In 1949, the illuminations were restored and three million visitors paid admission to the pier, the annual gate averaging 1.5 million people over the next ten years. In 1959, arsonists destroyed the derelict pavilion. Meanwhile, the pier railway was deteriorating, and by the end of the 1960s, steamers had put an end to their Southend service.

By the 1970s, the numbers of visitors to the pier had dropped alarmingly so a long-term £3 million restoration and repair programme was announced. However, as luck would have it, a fire destroyed the 1908 pier head on 29 July 1976 and caused £1.4 million damage. Another fire followed in 1977, and in the following year, the pier's rail track was declared unsafe and the trains were scrapped in 1982. The local council was all set to have the pier closed but Locorne Amusements came to the rescue and operated the pier on a trial basis. A rebuilding programme began in November 1984, including the construction of a 3ft-gauge diesel railway, which opened in September 1985. Disaster hit the pier on 30 June 1986 when the *MV Kings Abbey* sliced through the pier structure destroying the lifeboat slipway and leaving a 70ft gap.

Almost 100 years after the opening of the 'new' pier, a museum was opened beneath the shore station on 8 July 1989. Fire destroyed the bowling alley and badly damaged the railway on 7 June 1995 and put it out of action for a year. From June 2002, work began on restoring the area damaged by fire in 1976. Then, unbelievably, on 9 October 2005, yet another disastrous fire befell the pier. The old pier head dating from 1899 was destroyed, as were all its major facilities, including the arcade and historic railway station. A 130ft section of the pier was destroyed by the fire, with 65ft of it collapsing into the sea. It is estimated that the damage amounted to £10 million. Amazingly, the pier was reopened to visitors on 1 December and one of the trains was brought back into service.

RIGHT: A splendid 1950s view of the world's longest pier. *(English Heritage)*
FAR RIGHT: A fine Edwardian view of Southend Pier. *(Richard Riding collection)*
LEFT: This aerial view shows *PS Royal Eagle* at Southend pier head in 1947. *(English Heritage)*

SOUTHPORT 1860

Southport's pier has two claims for inclusion in the record books; it was the second structure of its kind to be built (Margate Jetty was the first) and it is the second longest pier in the country (Southend's being the longest). After the Southport Pier Company was formed in 1859, work went ahead on a 3,600ft pier designed by James Brunlees with Manchester contractors W & J Galloway in charge of the construction, while John Dixon was responsible for the piling. The pier's extreme length was to enable it to reach a deep-water channel to allow steamers to berth.

The pier was officially opened on 2 August 1860, having taken just twelve months to complete. At first it was very basic; there were few facilities and steamer passengers had to walk the half-mile to the shore. Between 1862-1863, waiting and refreshment rooms were added and a line of track laid down the centre of the deck for conveying luggage on man-powered trucks. Between 1864-1868, the pier was upgraded and extended to 4380ft. The pier neck was widened in order to run the rail track down one side, running cable-hauled cars capable of carrying passengers and luggage.

Like most piers, Southport received more than its fair share of disasters, most of them the result of severe weather. On 3 February 1889, the refreshment rooms were destroyed, and on 18 September 1897, the first pavilion burned down. After a new pavilion was opened in January 1902, the original pier entrance was replaced. By the 1920s, Southport was suffering similar problems to that of nearby New Brighton – the deep channels were gradually accumulating silt, which threatened to put the pier out of reach of steamers.

ABOVE: This Edwardian postcard view of the pier shows three 1905-rail cars operating as a train. *(Richard Riding collection)*
RIGHT: An aerial photograph taken of the shore end of Southport Pier on 20 August 1920. The tramway can be seen on the right hand side of the neck. *(English Heritage)*

Meanwhile, in 1936, ownership of the pier had passed to Southport Corporation who updated the tramway rolling stock.

Surprisingly Southport Pier was not sectioned during World War 2. However, it was closed to the public, and searchlights were installed to pick out German bombers on their way to Merseyside. Fires on 23 July 1933 and 22 June 1959 took their toll, reducing the pier's length to a 'mere' 3633ft. By the 1950s, the tramway's motive power had changed to diesel, with the eight-car *Silver Belle* train running from 1954 on a newly laid 60cm gauge track. Further changes to the pier took place in 1963 when a new bar and café were added. The 1902 pavilion was demolished and an amusement centre and other amenities developed.

During the 1990s, considerable uncertainty surrounded the pier and its future. It was losing money and rather than pay for urgent repair work, Sefton Council suggested demolishing the structure, a proposal quashed by a very narrow margin. The Southport 2000/Save the Pier group and the Southport Pier Trust were formed to raise funds for the pier's restoration. With money from the Heritage Lottery Fund and other sources, a two-phase restoration, including the construction of a pavilion housing an interpretation centre, was carried out between 1999 and 2003 at a cost of £7.2 million. Since August 2005, an 80-seat two-car pier tram has linked the pier head with the pavilion.

ABOVE: The fully restored pier showing the new Visitor Centre pictured in July 2003. *(Anthony Wills)*
LEFT: The limitations of early aerial cameras are obvious in this valiant attempt to capture the entire 4380ft pier in 1928. *(English Heritage)*

Southsea's Clarence Pier is unique in that it is considerably wider than it is long, being built parallel with the shore rather than projecting out to sea. Constructed from 1860-1861, the pier was opened by the Princess of Wales on 1 June 1861. It soon built up a reputation for good music performed in the large circular concert hall. Situated by the mouth of Portsmouth Harbour, it was well placed to attract steamer traffic, especially to the Isle of Wight across the Solent. From 1866, the Landport and Southsea Tramway ran from Portsmouth Town station right up to the pier to meet the ferries. In August 1882, the Prince of Wales, later King Edward VII, opened the Esplanade Theatre. The pier's deck received a concrete extension in 1905 whilst a concourse hall, shops and a café were introduced in 1932.

During World War 2, the pier was virtually destroyed on the night of 10 January 1941 in one of Portsmouth's heaviest air raids. The raiders, however, did not escape unscathed as at least two German bombers were shot down. There was no rush to rebuild the wrecked pier, with work commencing in 1953. The basic structure took six years to complete, the result being a completely new pier costing £250,000. The most striking feature was a 60ft steel tower designed by A. E. Cogswell & Sons of Portsmouth, which still stands today. Fittingly, on 1 June 1961, precisely 100 years after the opening of the original structure, Clarence Pier opened its gates once more to holidaymakers. It is currently billed as the largest amusement park on the south coast and is an unashamed 'candy floss' structure that fulfils its brief admirably.

ABOVE: An aerial view of *PS Balmoral* at Southsea Clarence Pier on 20 August 1939, just before the outbreak of war. *(English Heritage)*
LEFT: An Edwardian postcard view of trippers on the pier. *(Richard Riding collection)*
OPPOSITE: Another aerial view of the busy pier c.1930. *(Richard Riding collection)*

SOUTHSEA SOUTH PARADE 1879

Built to receive steamers on the Isle of Wight ferry services, Southsea's second pier was designed by G. Rale of Blackburn and built during 1875-1878 by Head Wrightson. The 1950ft structure was more of a landing stage than a pleasure pier and was opened by Prince Edward and Princess Saxe-Weimar in November 1879. At the time, the prince was Lieutenant Governor of the Garrison.

The privately owned pier was practically destroyed by fire on 19 July 1904, and for a period lay derelict, a mass of black ruins and twisted metal. It was taken over by the Portsmouth Corporation, which set about having a new pier erected on the site. Opened in 1908, the pier was designed by G. E. Smith and was markedly different to its predecessor. At 600ft, it was much shorter than the original structure but its wide decked area was designed to accommodate a number of substantial buildings. Perhaps mindful of what had destroyed the earlier pier, it was constructed with a concrete deck. The octagonal pier head had windscreens offering protection from virtually all directions, within which was built a bandstand, later joined by a small pavilion with a lounge and bar. At the shore end, a large pavilion housed a 1200-seat theatre (the 'Gaiety') and a hall that doubled as a café during the day and a dance hall at night.

For a long period, the pier was a commercial failure and was known as the 'White Elephant' by irate ratepayers; after all, it had cost a considerable £85,000 to build, the equivalent of £5 million today. However, its fortunes improved over the next 30 years. A craze for skating made the pier a popular venue, particularly for sailors who had made a speciality of skating backwards, causing collisions and multiple upsets. Having been built a mile further east from Portsmouth Harbour, closer to Southsea's main residential area, South Parade escaped the fate of Clarence Pier during World War 2, though it was breached and later used as a preparation area for the D-Day landings. It remained unscathed until 1967, when a fire damaged the theatre to such an extent that it was demolished the following year.

During the filming of the 'Pinball Wizard' sequence in Ken Russell's *Tommy* on 11 June 1974, it is reported that a spotlight set fire to drapes of the Gaiety Theatre, causing a conflagration that soon got out of control. Strong winds hampered the efforts of more than 100 firemen, but the pier was safely evacuated without casualties. In the following year, the pavilion was rebuilt at a cost of £500,000 in a vaguely Art Deco style and today the pier offers traditional amusements, bars and facilities for anglers.

RIGHT: An aerial view of the second pier, opened in 1908 and seen here in July 1958. *(English Heritage)*

OPPOSITE: An aerial view of the pier taken on a busy day in August 1932. *(English Heritage)*

SOUTHWOLD 1900

A late starter in the pier building stakes was the Suffolk coastal town of Southwold, a popular haunt for artists and an exclusive holiday resort. Although a popular call for steamers, the lack of facilities meant that passengers had to be rowed ashore: not a pleasant prospect in poor weather. Also, the Coast Development Company, operators of the Belle steamers between London Bridge and Great Yarmouth, often bypassed Southwold. In due course, the company set its sights on Southwold, and in August 1899, it announced that a wooden pier costing £9,000 would be built at the eastern end of a street (Pier Avenue) to be in operation by the following summer.

Designed by W. Jeffrey, the first pile was driven in on 2 October 1899, and unusually, there was no formal opening of the pier when the first Belle steamer berthed in June 1900. The 810ft pier was little more than a landing stage with few amusements, but at least steamers were calling in rather than steaming by as in the past. After the Coast Development Company was wound up around 1922, the pier was taken over by the Amusement Equipment Company Ltd. Steamers continued to ply between London and Great Yarmouth until the T-shaped landing stage succumbed to a storm in December 1933. By this time, Belle Steamers Ltd had ceased business (the company was dissolved in October 1931) and the landing stage was never replaced. In 1936, in an effort to attract visitors, the new owners replaced the original wooden buildings at the pier entrance with the typical two-storey 1930s structure that exists today.

Southwold Pier was sectioned as an invasion precaution in 1940 and was then further damaged by a drifting mine. Repairs costing £30,000 were completed in 1948 but the ailing structure became the victim of storms.

BELOW: This 1920 aerial photograph of Southwold Pier shows the original pier head. (*English Heritage*)

The middle of the pier was breached in October 1955 and a drifting vessel reduced what was left of the structure to a stump in February 1979. There the story of Southwold Pier should have ended had not the Iredale family arrived on the scene. After acquiring the freehold in 1987, the entrance building was rejuvenated and reopened in December 1988. In 1999, work began on rebuilding the pier to its current length of 620ft. Four pavilions were erected encompassing a bar, restaurant, mini-museum of pier history and unusual amusements. The pier's T-shaped landing stage was restored and the 'new' pier was officially opened by the Duke of Gloucester on 3 July 2001 – a real credit to the vision and determination of Chris and Helen Iredale.

RIGHT: The Iredale's rebuilding of the pier as completed in 2001.
FAR RIGHT: A comical attraction on Southwold Pier is Tim Hunkin's bawdy water clock where two boys drop their trousers and have a pee every half hour!
(Both: Richard Riding collection)
BELOW: Another aerial view from 1950 showing the entrance building erected in 1936.
(English Heritage)

The Isle of Purbeck in Dorset is noted for its stone, used to pave city streets or in the fabric of important buildings. Most of the quarries are a mile or so from Swanage Bay from where the blocks of stone were shipped to London and elsewhere. For generations it was taken out to waiting boats in carts, a dangerous and time-consuming process. In the late 1850s, a Capt W. S. Moorsom devised the idea of laying a tramway from the quarries down to a purpose-built wooden pier from which the quarried stone could be loaded aboard. Royal consent for such a structure was given in August 1859 and the Swanage Pier & Tramway Company was formed.

John Walton was given the task of building the 750ft pier and it was opened for traffic in September 1861 at a cost of £6,000. As time went by, steamers from Bournemouth and elsewhere made increasing use of the pier, but with the introduction of the railway to Swanage in 1885, the stone trade switched to rail. As the 19th century drew to a close, the pier was showing its age and was unable to cope with the level of steamship activity. A new pier was designed by Richard St George of Westminster and construction began in November 1895 under Alfred Thorne. The 642ft wooden structure cost £10,000 and was a no frills landing stage supported on 170 greenheart timber piles running immediately adjacent to the old pier. It was fully operational by Easter 1897, and during the holiday no fewer than 10,000 people arrived at the resort by steamer.

The old pier deteriorated rapidly and up to World War 1 served as a coaling and

ABOVE: The pier head and landing stage on completion of full restoration in 1998. *(Richard Riding collection)*

RIGHT: This aerial view of the Swanage piers was taken in October 1935 and shows how both structures share the same entrance approach. *(English Heritage)*

overnight berth for Cosens & Company's steamers. After brief use by the Swanage Swimming Club, the pier finally rotted away and only lines of stumps indicate where it once stood. By the 1920s, all was not well with the second pier. The dreaded gribble of the genus *Limnoria*, a grey wood-boring marine crustacean, had been tucking into the wooden piles for years. In 1927, the piles were encased in concrete ensuring their survival for a further 60 years. With the declaration of war in 1939, the pier was breached at its entrance and it was not until 1948 that this section was restored in concrete.

For the next 15 or so years, paddle steamers regularly plied across the bay to and from Bournemouth, the Isle of Wight and Weymouth. However, this came to an end on 24 September 1966 when PS *Embassy* entered the record books as the last paddle steamer to use the pier. Or was she? In time, the pier began a slow but steady decline and would have probably gone the same way as its neighbour had it not been purchased by Durrant Developments Ltd who planned to restore the pier. Unfortunately, the company went bankrupt before work could begin and the Swanage Pier Trust acquired the structure in 1994. The trust managed to raise £1 million and a full restoration programme took place during 1996-1998. The pier was officially reopened in July 1998 and looks just as impressive as it did in its glory days. The icing on the cake are the regular visits by PS *Waverley* during the summer months.

BELOW: An aerial view of both piers taken in 1947, showing marked deterioration of the old pier and work taking place repairing the breached portion of the 'new' pier. *(English Heritage)*

The years 1865-1871 must have given engineer Joseph William Wilson much satisfaction for all four of his piers (Bognor, Hunstanton, Teignmouth and Westward Ho!) were opened during this period. His design for Teignmouth, as with his other piers, was a simple, elegant structure of wood and iron. Four eastern-influenced pagodas stood at the entrance and seats ran the entire 700ft length of the pier to where a landing stage was erected to receive steamers. The Chairman of the Local Board performed the opening ceremony in 1867. The pier's main claim to fame is that it was the first seaside pier in Britain to feature coin-operated 'What the Butler Saw' machines.

The pier had already had two owners by the time it was acquired by Arthur H. Dendy in 1887. He had the extraordinary notion of moving the entire pier to nearby Paignton! Fortunately for Teignmouth, apart from the cost involved, it was considered that the pier would not travel well and it remained *in situ*. By this time, a 250ft pavilion had been built at the shore end and the 300-seat Castle Pavilion was constructed at the pier head. A landing stage was added and connected to the pier head by a 35ft footbridge. The pier was subject to the usual bouts of storms, first in 1894 and then again on 3-4 January 1908, when the protective sea wall collapsed in front of the pier, badly damaging the entrance building and kiosks. In 1940, a 60ft breach was made and the landing stage removed. Although the pier received a few near misses during the war, it survived the conflict and damage was restored.

During the 1950s, the pier was upgraded to the tune of £20,000, and in the early 1960s, its length was reduced with the removal of the landing stage. Complete refurbishment took place in the 1970s. In 2001, the family-owned pier faced closure when fire authorities and Health and Safety informed the owners that the pier failed to meet current safety laws. Officials insisted that walkways be added to either side of the pier's shore end building, which entailed expensive widening of the pier at this point. The work was carried out in 2002 and involved driving in fourteen 24-metre long piles into the bedrock. The Brenner family have owned and managed the pier as Grand Pier (Teignmouth) Ltd since 1961.

RIGHT: An aerial view of Teignmouth Pier taken on 14 August 1939. *(English Heritage)*

RIGHT: An Edwardian postcard view of the pier. *(Richard Riding collection)*
BOTTOM RIGHT: An aerial photograph showing Castle Hill, Tenby Royal Victoria Pier and the lifeboat station taken in 1921. *(English Heritage)*

We hesitated in including Tenby's pier, not generally regarded as a pleasure pier, in this section, but the aerial photograph tipped the balance! Strictly speaking, the structure was only a glorified approach with three bays of steel arches leading down to a 200ft landing stage built to receive steamers from seaside resorts in Somerset, North Devon and, of course, South Wales. The pier was built in 1897 and then extended in 1899, when it was officially opened by the Duke of York and named Tenby Royal Victoria Pier. In addition to receiving steamers, it was a popular venue for concerts performed at the pier head and was also favoured by anglers. As can be seen in the aerial photograph, the pier was adjacent to the lifeboat jetty. Demolition of the pier began in 1946 and the task was finally completed in 1953.

TORQUAY PRINCESS 1890

If it were not for the concrete groin structure that leads off left at right angles to the pier head, Torquay's Princess Pier would look more like a conventional seaside pier. As it stands, it could easily be overlooked as one side of a harbour, which explains why a number of previous books on piers overlooked it. The pier started out in 1890 as a simple concrete groin, and it was to be a further four years before a conventional steel lattice girder and wooden structure were added. A wooden landing stage followed in 1906. Around this time, the Islander concert pavilion was built on the pier head. The building was badly damaged by a fire in 1974 and was later demolished.

The pier appears to have had little in the way of amusements but has attracted visitors for whom continuous seating is provided along both sides. During the 1950s, major repair work was carried out replacing half of the pier head substructure. A shelter was built in 1965 and in 1978, it was discovered that much of the pier's steel subframe had corroded and the other half of the pier head needed replacing. This complex engineering work was carried out over the ensuing months at a cost of £255,000 and the pier reopened in 1979.

ABOVE: A between-the-wars view of Torquay's Princess Pier showing the Islander pavilion at the seaward end. *(Richard Riding collection)*
RIGHT: This aerial view of the pier was taken on 7 September 1928 and clearly shows the layout of the structure. Without the concrete groin, running from the pier head to the bottom right of the photograph, it would resemble a typical seaside pier. *(English Heritage)*

Many coastal resorts on the Isle of Wight were keen to cash in on the steamer trips from the mainland and Totland Bay was no exception. Plans were set in motion in 1879 and S. H. and S. W. Yockney designed a 450ft wooden structure of light girder framework on a wooden deck supported by cast-iron piles. Construction was completed by March 1880 and though primarily a landing stage, the facilities included a pier head shelter and shore end amusement pavilion.

Before long, a connecting service for steamers plying between Lymington and Yarmouth was established and within a few years, steamers came from further afield putting Totland Bay well and truly on the tourist map. This continued until the outbreak of World War 1 when ferry services were discontinued for a brief period. After the war, the pier slowly deteriorated and by 1927, ferry services had stopped calling, though pleasure steamers continued to use the pier until 1931.

The ailing pier was sectioned on the outbreak of World War 2, and with the return of peace, repairs were carried out – a number of iron piles were replaced with wood and a pier head shelter was erected. The pier was reopened on 17 June 1951 and the occasion was marked by the arrival of *PS Lorna Doone*, the first steamer to visit for 20 years. In the early 1970s, the pier was sold to Trinity House for £10,000, becoming the base for pilot boats to meet liners and assist with navigation through the Needles Channel to Southampton. In 1975, the National Physical Laboratory used the pier to gather data on wave and weather properties, and from this point, the ownership of the deteriorating structure changed several times.

By 1980, the pier was officially declared to be unsafe and was closed. The Great Storm of 1987 wrecked the amusement arcade though this was rebuilt. In 1992, the pier was sold for just £1,000 and its new owner Henry Leeson embarked upon a restoration programme, which was hampered by vandalism. Today, the pier is owned by Derek Barran, and although in somewhat shaky condition, it remains open to visitors by appointment.

LEFT: An aerial view of the pier taken in April 1972 during which period it was under the ownership of Trinity House. *(English Heritage)*
BELOW: Totland Bay Pier pictured between the wars. *(Richard Riding collection)*

Had the fates been kinder, Ventnor could have had an eye-catching double pier arrangement. Engineered for the Ventnor Pier and Harbour Company by local man J. Saunders, work began in 1863. The partially finished western arm was opened in June but in October 1864, the uncompleted eastern arm was badly damaged by gales. Further storm damage in January 1867 put paid to the project and John Burt purchased the western pier for £400.

Undeterred by events, the Ventnor Pier & Esplanade Company was formed in 1870 and the Royal Victoria Pier was built in stages over a period of ten years. After two months of operation, the entire pier was wrecked in a storm in November 1881 and it was back to square one. Saunders designed a 650ft pier with a shield shaped head and contractors Trehearne & Company of Battersea began work in late 1885. The £12,000 structure was opened by Sir Richard Webster MP on 19 October 1887 and soon gained popularity with promenaders. A £980 pavilion replaced a temporary building at the pier head and a bandstand was erected at the pavilion entrance in 1913. Though concert parties carried on during World War 1, steamer services were postponed until 1919.

The pier was sectioned during World War 2; 100ft of the structure was broken up and thrown into the sea. After the war, the pier was condemned following a survey. Attempts to receive compensation from the ministry finally succeeded and ninety per cent of the restoration costs was met, the local council having to find £15,000 for the landing stage and entrance buildings. Although some components from the original pier were incorporated, including much of the landing stage, contractors Messrs Wall Brothers built a virtually new 683ft pier with a reinforced 12,000 square foot concrete pier head. The neck had nine 30ft-long glass windscreens whilst the new pier head featured an entertainment complex with bars and a sun deck. The official opening of 'the most modern pier in Britain' took place on 28 May 1955, though steamers had been visiting since May 1953.

By 1967, the landing stage needed repairing and with the reduction in the steamer trade, only a part was restored. A structural survey in 1981 revealed that further repair work would cost £750,000. To make matters worse, a fire broke out and caused serious damage; what was left of the landing stage was demolished soon after. With the pier in a critical condition, various schemes were put forwards for a complete restoration or a replacement. However, legal wrangles between the pier's lessee and the local council resulted in deadlock. Fresh hopes were raised with the formation of the Ventnor Town Trust, which was interested in acquiring the pier and restoring it. South Wight Borough Council offered to transfer ownership if the trust could raise £1 million for the complete restoration. Sadly, public support was lacking and the pier was demolished in 1993.

LEFT: An aerial view of the pier taken in 1933. *(English Heritage)*
OPPOSITE: Ignoring the wartime breach, this 1947 aerial view seems to show the pier in good condition. However, the structure was condemned a year later and in 1950, work began to build a new pier. *(English Heritage)*

Walton's first pier was built in mid-1830 and was the fourth example in England, following Ryde (1813), Brighton Chain (1823) and Southend (1829). The 150ft pier was built to receive steamers but was too short for its intended purpose and in 1839, it was extended a further 200ft. By 1848, the pier had grown to 680ft in length but still could only be reached by steamers at high tide. In April 1859, work began on another pier close by. Civil engineer Peter Bruff had arrived in Walton in 1855 and set about changing the town's fortunes, as he would do with nearby Clacton a few years later. This included bringing the railway to Walton in 1867 and the proposed construction of a new pier.

Cochrane & Son began work on the new 530ft long pier in April 1869. However, Bruff's design suffered from the same problem as its rival: it stood in shallow water and at low tides, steamer passengers had to transfer to small boats to get ashore. Meanwhile, the owner of the Marine Hotel overlooking the new pier was not pleased with Bruff's plans and raised money to have the original pier lengthened by a further 800ft. Unfortunately, severe storms damaged the lengthy structure during the winter of 1880-1881, and unable to afford the necessary repair work, the owners were forced to have it demolished. The new pier stayed open for business, but with the limited access it provided for steamers and with trippers arriving by rail, there was insufficient income to pay for renewal and repairs to the deteriorating structure.

Bruff sold the pier and by 1898, ownership passed to the Coast Development Company (CDC), which financed the complete rebuilding of the pier to a length of 2600ft. This necessitated the installation of a single-line electric tramway to transport passengers and baggage to the pier head, with one motorcar and two open-sided trailers each with bench seating for 32 passengers. A new

ABOVE: This aerial photograph of Walton-on-the-Naze Pier was taken in August 1938. *(English Heritage)*
LEFT: An early postcard view showing the single-track electric railway and the pier head pavilion. *(Richard Riding collection)*

three-berth pier head was built and a 750-seat pavilion, restaurant and shooting gallery were introduced. After CDC folded, new owners took over the pier in 1915, and in 1927, the famous Sea Spray Lounge was built at the shore end. In 1936, the Goss family who formed the New Walton Pier Company Ltd acquired the pier.

Before it could be breached as an invasion precaution during World War 2, the pier was severely damaged by a fire on 30 May 1942. It was rebuilt by Walton-on-the-Naze Urban District Council and reopened in 1948. A single 2ft gauge line laid for use by the contractors was later employed to carry passengers and continued in use until 1977. In December 1978, a storm caused a 100ft breach at the seaward end cutting off access to the Walton lifeboat. The damage was repaired and today the pier is still owned by New Walton Pier Company Ltd. A large aircraft hangar-like amusement arcade is located at the pier entrance; those looking for comparative peace and quiet will find it with the anglers at the pier head, where a new lifeboat berth was opened in May 2005.

ABOVE: Between-the-wars view showing the pier tramway cars in their siding. *(Richard Riding collection)*
RIGHT: An aerial view of Walton Pier taken on 30 June 1961. *(English Heritage)*

WESTON-SUPER-MARE BIRNBECK 1867

Birnbeck Island lies about 1000ft across the water from Weston and in days past the local fishermen caught mackerel and sprats and dried their nets there. The first attempt to bridge the gap came in 1847 when work began on a suspension bridge designed by James Dredge. The project was plagued by problems; a masons' strike and then a storm that damaged the work already completed, after which Dredge was declared bankrupt. Twenty years were to pass before the island was successfully bridged.

The task fell to Eugenius Birch who designed a pier that would cope with the 46ft rise and fall of the notorious Severn tides. The 1350ft structure was made from pre-fabricated parts supplied and erected by the Isca Iron Foundry at Newport, Gwent. The foundation stone was laid on 28 October 1864 by 8-year-old Cecil Smyth-Pigott who also opened the pier on 6 June 1867. During its first three months of the pier's opening, 120,000 people had visited it. Birnbeck Island soon became a popular calling point for steamers, particularly those of P. & A. Campbell, resulting in various improvements being carried out on the structure to make it useable in low and high tides.

Originally the pier had a small pavilion and a 90ft concrete jetty, replaced in 1872 by a 250ft wooden structure on the north side of the pier. On 26 December 1897, fire destroyed many of the pier's buildings; these were replaced by July the following year. A low water jetty was built on the southwest side of the pier but both this and the north jetty were seriously damaged during a gale in 1903. During the previous year a new lifeboat house, with the longest slipway in the country, was constructed on the south side of the pier. By this time, work had commenced on Weston Grand Pier a mile to the south of Birnbeck, and after it

ABOVE: A postcard view of the pier c.1910. *(Richard Riding collection)*
RIGHT: This fascinating aerial photograph was taken at low tide on 30 June 1923. In the foreground is the dilapidated low water jetty, which was dismantled soon after. *(English Heritage)*

was opened in June 1904, Birnbeck was referred to as the Old Pier. Perhaps it was the anticipated competition from the new pier that was responsible for the arrival of the Birnbeck water chute and Flying Machine, both installed in 1905.

The pier remained open throughout World War 1, but during World War 2, was taken over by the admiralty and was known as HMS *Birnbeck* during the duration of the conflict. The pier was used for experiments with new weaponry, and although it escaped being sectioned, it was badly damaged by a friendly aircraft. An Avro Lancaster bomber had been ordered to drop a large bomb-shaped lump of concrete as close to the pier as possible – and one can only wonder why. And yes, you've guessed it; the concrete bomb hit the pier and flattened an engineering shed causing much damage to the structure!

The Birnbeck Pier Company sold the pier to P & A Campbell in 1962, by which time the steamer trade was dwindling. In 1972, Jim Critchley purchased the pier for around £50,000 but grand plans for the pier's development came to nothing. The structure received Grade II listing status in 1974 and the following year was up for auction, but the reserve price of £150,000 was not reached. After several other ownerships and unfulfilled plans for restoration, the pier was closed on safety grounds in 1994. In August 2007 owners Urban Splash (South West) launched an international architectural competition to design a 'residential community' on the pier, to include dozens of apartments and a hotel. Pier purists may not like the idea of converting a pier in this way, but at least it offers the possibility of preservation in an innovative way.

ABOVE: By the first decade of the 20th century, the pier had acquired a flying machine and water chute. (*Richard Riding collection*)

LEFT: In contrast to the earlier aerial photo, this view from June 1939 was taken at high tide. The pier head is much less cluttered – gone are the water chute and switchback railway. (*English Heritage*)

WESTON-SUPER-MARE GRAND 1904

Nearly four decades were to pass before Weston-super-Mare became a two-pier town, and although plans were laid as far back as 1880, it took a further 14 years before the Grand materialised, financed by a group of Cardiff businessmen. Designed by R. Munroe, the 1080ft structure was built by Mayoh & Hayley of London, the first pile being driven by local MP R. E. Dickinson on 7 November 1903. Construction only took seven months and the pier was officially opened on 12 June 1904. Included in the £120,000 cost was a 2,000-seat pavilion theatre at the pier head, shops, cafés and a bandstand.

Within a couple of years of opening a low-water landing stage had been completed, bringing the pier's total length to 2580ft; the original plan was to extend to a length of 6600ft! The intention had been to run a regular steamer service to Cardiff, but the tricky tide conditions and strong currents deterred vessels from mooring at the stage. By 1918, all but 120ft of the landing stage had been dismantled and Weston Grand concentrated on amusements and left nearby Birnbeck to cater for the steamer trade. Tragedy struck on 13 January 1930 when the pavilion burned down. In the aftermath, the pier head was enlarged to accommodate a new glass-roofed pavilion. In keeping with the times, the pavilion housed a funfair rather than a theatre.

In July 1946, ownership of the Grand passed to A. Brenner and has remained in the family ever since. After the entrance was modernised in 1970, the pier achieved listed status in 1974. Ever modernising and keeping up with amusement trends, the Grand opened a new £250,000 bowling alley in 1993. During the following year, a further £350,000 was spent on building a two-storey fun house and a Ferris wheel (the pier was re-decked during this period). A rail-less train has become a popular feature in recent years. Today, the Grand flourishes under the expert management of Roy Brenner and his team. In complete contrast, nearby Birnbeck, built on the other side of town, has lain derelict for many years.

LEFT: The pier's official opening: 12 June 1904. *(Richard Riding collection)*
ABOVE: An aerial view of the pier head and original pavilion taken in October 1928.
OPPOSITE: This aerial view of the Grand Pier was taken on 13 August 1939.
(Both: English Heritage)

WEYMOUTH BANDSTAND 1939

When construction of Weymouth's Bandstand pier began, there were complaints from the locals claiming that it would spoil the beautiful sweep of the bay. The design was opened up to competition by the Royal Institute of British Architects and from 26 entries, V. J. Venning's was chosen. Built using some 3000 tons of concrete, the 200ft pier followed in the tradition of other 'Modernist' seaside buildings such as the De La Warr Pavilion at Bexhill-on-Sea, its streamlined curves being typical of the time. The entrance building led to an open-air venue over the water featuring a stage at the seaward end. It was an attractive building when viewed from any angle, but one where practicality took second place to 'style'. No fixed seating was provided and whilst there was room for 2400 people, only 800 were under cover from the elements. In the event of rain, there was often an undignified rush for the covered sides of the auditorium. Subsequent plans to roof over this fair-weather building came to nothing.

The bandstand was opened on 25 May 1939 and within months the country had declared war on Germany. Unsurprisingly, there was not enough pier to be sectioned! During the 1950s and 1960s, the bandstand was a popular venue: Ted Heath & His Music played there in July 1958. Other entertainments included dancing, wrestling and Miss Weymouth contests. During the 1970s, further amenities included a restaurant and gift shop in addition to the usual amusements. Interestingly, in the 1980s, it was cheaper to hire a deckchair on the pier (10p) than on the beach (30p)!

By the mid-1980s, the bandstand was proving too costly to maintain (perhaps they should have been charging more for deckchairs!) and it was decided that it should be blown up. Someone with a spark of imagination came up with the idea of holding a national competition, the two winners of which would press the button! Two sisters from Birmingham, aged 11 and 14, carried out every child's dream in May 1986. Straddling the beach and promenade, the entrance building is still in existence; the front of the building has been restored to its original Art Deco style and the current owner hopes to restore the remainder of the pier in due course.

ABOVE RIGHT AND RIGHT: Two shots of Weymouth Bandstand shortly after it opened in 1939. *(English Heritage; Richard Riding collection)*

Various dates have been assigned to the origins of the earliest pier at Weymouth, some as far back as 1812. However, the present structure came into existence circa 1840 as an extension to the esplanade and was called the Pile Pier. In 1857, the railway reached Weymouth and ran on to terminate at the pier entrance. As a result, the pier was lengthened in 1859-1860, the curved wooden extension having a circular pier head with a small pavilion. This soon became the principal departure point of Weymouth-based Cosen's steamers. After the Weymouth and Channel Island Steam Packet Company Ltd was formed in 1867, a cargo stage was added in 1877, followed by a new passenger stage/baggage hall during 1888-1889.

The pier had been little more than a glorified landing stage but a 1100-seat pier pavilion was opened on reclaimed land adjacent to the pier entrance on 21 December 1908. Costing £13,573 to build, it staged drama, pantomimes and musicals and marked a significant move towards attracting the traditional holidaymaker to the pier. Great changes took place during the early 1930s when the original wooden pier was replaced with a 1,300ft concrete structure and divided into halves. Whilst retaining the promenade area to the north, the south side was developed further to handle three cargo vessels and two pleasure steamers simultaneously. The cost of this development amounted to £120,000. HRH the Prince of Wales was flown down from Windsor for the official opening on 13 July 1933, but narrowly missed the celebrations when his aircraft had to land at Swanage, the journey being completed by car.

During World War 2, the pavilion was closed to the public but was used for a period to shelter Belgian refugees. Renamed the Ritz, it reopened on 19 May 1950, but four years later, a workman's blowlamp caused it to burn down within an hour on 13 April 1954 in Weymouth's biggest blaze since the war. The Ritz Palm Court ballroom, built on the site of an Edwardian skating room and adjacent to the Ritz was untouched by the raging inferno. On 14 July 1960, the new Pavilion Theatre, incorporating the Ocean Room ballroom, was opened on the same site. Though damaged by fire in 1993, it operates today as the Alexandra Garden Theatre. In 2005, plans were announced for a spectacular £89 million redevelopment of the pier including a hotel, theatres, ferry terminal and 150-berth marina.

LEFT: An aerial view of the pavilion and railway in 1936. *(English Heritage)*

Unlike a number of piers mentioned in this book, Worthing Pier endured most of its major disasters within its first 70 years or so, since when its history has been comparatively uneventful. One of the earliest traditional seaside piers on the south coast, the 960ft structure was officially opened in April 1862 having taken less than a year to build. Initially there was little in the way of amenities apart from a single entrance kiosk and a landing stage. The pier quickly became popular and two kiosks designed by Alfred Crouch were erected at the entrance in 1884. Major improvements were made in 1888 when the width of the 16ft wide deck was doubled and the 650-seat Southern Pavilion was built at the pier head; the total cost being £12,000. The new look pier was reopened by Viscount Hampden on 1 July 1889, no fewer than 7000 paying to visit on that day alone. The landing stage proved popular with steamers but its use was restricted to high tide. There were plans to extend the pier but even by doubling its length, the water's depth would have only increased by a further 6ft.

Work was about to begin on a new pavilion in 1913 when disaster struck on the evening of Easter Monday. The pier was subjected to gale force winds during the day which persisted through the evening whilst a concert performance was taking place. Unnerved by the storm, the audience left the concert and made for the safety of the shore as the musicians played on – shades of the *Titanic*! Just after midnight, the pier shuddered and the decking between the pavilion and the shore collapsed and fell into the sea. The marooned pavilion was nicknamed Easter Island by the locals and proved to be a popular with tourists and photographers – shades of Brighton West!

RIGHT: An aerial view of Worthing pier taken in 1935. *(English Heritage)*
BELOW: An Edwardian view of the pier showing the original entrance kiosks. *(Richard Riding collection)*

RIGHT: This aerial view of 'Easter Island' was taken on 6 September 1913 and is one of the earliest aerial photographs taken of a pier. *(Richard Riding collection)*
BELOW: This dramatic low-level aerial view of the Southern Pavilion was taken on 27 August 1933, just two weeks before its destruction by fire. *(English Heritage)*

In double-quick time, the pier was repaired, strengthened and reopened by The Lord Mayor of London on 29 May 1914.

Ownership of the pier passed to Worthing Corporation in 1920. In addition to the £19,000 purchase price, a further £40,000 was spent on more repair work and a new entrance pavilion resembling a jelly mould and designed by Adshead & Ramsey, which opened in June 1926. On 10 September 1933, a disastrous fire wiped out the Southern Pavilion. The first indication of the impending fire was when smoke was seen billowing out from under the landing stage. Inexplicably, the alarm was not raised for a further 20 minutes.

Within half an hour the pavilion was gutted and it was fortunate that there were no injuries. A new £18,000 pavilion was built in the streamlined '30s style and still stands today. During 1937, windshields were erected along the length of the pier and a central amusement pavilion was built.

As with most south and east coast piers, Worthing was sectioned as an invasion precaution. A 120ft breach was blown on the shore side of the Southern Pavilion, and from 1942, the pier was used as a reception centre for troops. After the war, the shoreward section of the pier was opened by June 1946, but a shortage of steel necessary to repair parts of the structure meant that the pier was not fully opened until April 1949. During 1979-1982, the shoreward end pavilion was upgraded as an entertainments centre.

BELOW: 'Easter Island' seen from the shore in 1913. The pier was repaired and in operation within 14 months. *(Richard Riding collection)*

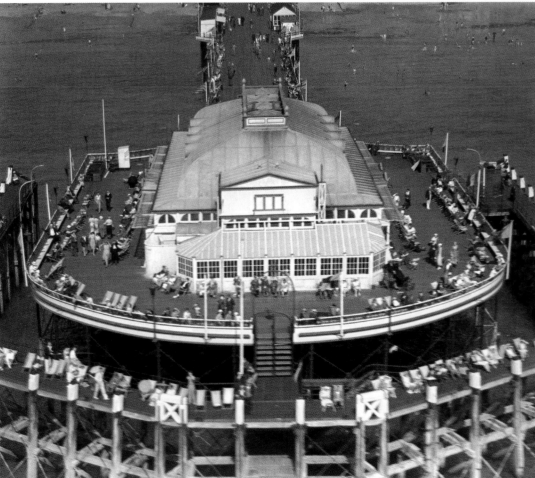

YARMOUTH (IOW) 1876

Although there were plans for a pier to be built at Yarmouth as early as 1870, it took some time for all parties concerned to agree upon its exact location. The railway company wanted it to be from the north side of the castle so that trains could be brought close to it, but the War Office would not entertain the idea. Finally in 1874, permission was granted to build the pier from the shore at the bottom of Bank Street. Construction of the 685ft wooden pier was handled by Denham & Jenvey of Freshwater and was completed in time for its official opening on 19 July 1876 by the Mayor of Yarmouth.

The pier had only been open for a few weeks before a 150ft section was damaged by the steamer *Prince Leopold* in near perfect conditions. Anxious for the steamer company's patronage of their pier, Yarmouth Corporation apologised for the damage! Steamer services stepped up after the railway was extended to Lymington Pier across the water in 1884, with regular services to Yarmouth commencing the same year. A table of tolls from 1896 reveals some interesting rates: promenaders paid 1d, the same rate for passengers landing or embarking. Taking a bicycle onto the pier cost 2d, whilst a corpse would cost the bearers three shillings, reinforcing the old adage that death and taxes are unavoidable.

During 1927, a small pavilion, waiting room and offices were added, and in 1931, the pier came under the jurisdiction of the Pier & Harbour Commissioners. Fishing from the pier was banned soon after, those caught doing so being threatened with a fine of 40 shillings. With the increase in demand for transporting cars across the Solent, a slipway was built adjacent to the pier, which effectively siphoned away steamer business. The pier became a Grade II listed building in 1975, but by 1980, was beginning to show its age and required complete restoration – the Harbour Commissioners sought permission to have Yarmouth Pier demolished, though this was refused. Since 1983, close to £1 million has been spent on the pier and given that it is constructed almost entirely of wood, the periodic maintenance costs will remain high. However, it remains popular and enjoys frequent visits by PS *Waverley* and MV *Balmoral*.

LEFT: An aerial photo of the pier taken on 5 September 1938. *(English Heritage)*

British Seaside Piers

Appendix

The majority of the piers in this appendix disappeared long before the era of commercial aerial photography. However, there is a handful that still exist today which should, by rights, have featured in the main gazetteer. However, we were unable to find suitable aerial views within the archives we consulted.

ABERAVON 1898-1964

Although Aberavon Pier was originally conceived as a breakwater, it served as a pleasure pier between 1902 and 1940. Constructed of timber by the Port Talbot Railway & Docks Company in 1898 and named the North Pier, the 900ft structure was acquired by Aberavon District Council in 1902. By adding turnstiles and railings, the structure became a pleasure pier and was popular with promenaders. However, there were no amusements.

During the 1920s, the pier suffered damage from severe weather and had to be strengthened and repaired. By the end of World War 2, during which time the pier was closed, it had become derelict. The British Transport Commission invested in re-decking the pier, but by the 1960s, its structure had fallen into disrepair once more, and during 1964, a £250,000 repair programme had to be undertaken. Many wooden sections were replaced with concrete and after the work was complete, the pier once more took on the appearance of a breakwater. Its current owners remind visitors that it 'is not designed or intended for use by the public.'

ALDEBURGH 1878-1909

Plans for a pier to be erected at Aldeburgh were first mooted in 1864 but the idea fizzled out and it was not until the formation of the Aldborough Pier and Improvement Company in 1875 that plans were laid. Designed by Thomas Cargill, the cast-iron structure was to have been 561ft in length with a pentagonal pier head. Work got underway late in 1876 but was postponed in March 1878 after half the structure had been completed. The pier company went bust and there were insufficient funds to complete its construction.

In December 1881, the pier was auctioned and reportedly sold to the original contractor for £400. In the following year, John H. Fuller acquired the pier. Fuller had plans to complete the pier but was frustrated by a lack of funds. In addition, the pier had been damaged after the steamer *Winifred* collided with the structure. The pier was demolished on the authority of the local council and all that remains are a few piles embedded in the beach.

FAR LEFT: Aberavon in use as a pleasure pier c.1904. *(Richard Riding collection)*

BELOW: Though of poor quality this is the only known photograph of the half-completed Aldeburgh pier. *(Richard Riding collection)*

BRIGHTON CHAIN 1823-1896

For a brief period, until the night of 4-5 December 1896, Brighton could boast three piers. On the formation of the Brighton Pier Company in 1821, Capt Samuel Brown RN, designer of the Leith Trinity Chain pier then being built, began work on a similar design some 1134ft in length consisting of four 260ft spans carried on a total of 70 Norwegian pine piles. Costing £30,000, the Chain Pier was opened on 25 November 1823. Thereafter, the pier attracted a steady stream of visitors and during two Sundays in 1824, more than 3,000 people used it. Attractions on the pier included a floating bath at the pier head, refreshment and souvenir shops in the towers, numerous telescopes, an excellent reading room and a camera obscura, which was added in 1831.

The pier flourished for its first ten years after which storms began to take their toll. On 15 October 1833, the pier was struck by lightning causing considerable fire damage. Another storm on 29 November 1836 destroyed the third span of the pier whilst the structure survived a waterspout on 5 August 1848. A more serious threat to the pier was the opening of the West Pier in October 1866. Whereas the Chain Pier had been designed as a landing stage, the new pier was for promenading and (later) entertainment. In 1891, ownership of the Chain Pier passed to the Marine Palace & Pier Company, owners of Brighton's third pier, the Palace. One of the conditions of the Board of Trade was that as soon as the Palace Pier was completed the Chain Pier should be removed. The old structure was considered unsafe and was closed on 9 October 1896 and offered for sale. The pier head was now leaning seven feet out of perpendicular.

ALUM BAY (IOW) 1887-c.1927

By the time work began on a wooden pier at Alum Bay in 1869, there had already been two landing stages at this western Isle of Wight resort. They were small and quite unsuitable for the growing number of steamers calling, so J. White of Cowes for the Needles and Alum Bay Pier Company erected a more substantial wooden structure. This in turn was replaced by a 370ft long iron pier built by I. Saunders for £2,135. The broad-headed pier was opened on 5 August 1887 and the resort benefited from the influx of day-trippers right up to World War 1.

By 1924, the steamer trade had disappeared and the pier quickly deteriorated to such an extent that it was closed the following year. The pier company went into liquidation in 1926 and during the following year, one of the pier's spans collapsed putting all but the shore end out of action. By this time the pier had been acquired by Alfred Isaacs and remained in the family's ownership for many years. During World War 2, Alum Bay Pier and the surrounding area was used as a military practice area and looked like a battlefield when hostilities ended in 1945. The derelict pier continued to deteriorate until there was little of it remaining by the late 1950s.

On the night of 4-5 December, a violent storm caused the pier to collapse into the sea. Some of the baulks of timber were carried west and damaged both the West Pier and the uncompleted Palace Pier. On 11 December, the flotsam was collected into 150 lots and offered for sale: an ignominious end for one of only three suspension piers to be built in Britain.

BURNHAM-ON-SEA 1911

As Burnham-on-Sea's pier barely puts a foot in the water, it is often considered not to be a fully-fledged pier but merely a beach pavilion on piles. But size isn't everything, and as we have included Weymouth Bandstand, we felt we should not ignore the structure at Burnham. Built of concrete between 1911-1914, the 'pier' was reported to have been used for shipping for a short period. It was taken over by Harry Parkin in 1968, by which time the pavilion was derelict. The owner restored the building and the pier offers all the usual facilities and amusements.

COATHAM 1873-1899

Regarded as one of the most obscure of Britain's seaside piers, Coatham's ill-fated pier, like most on the Yorkshire coast, was short-lived. After formation of the Coatham Pier Company, work started on the structure in 1871. Its planned length was to have been 2,000ft and this had almost been reached in December 1874 when disaster struck. A severe storm forced both the brig *Griffen* and the schooner *Corrymbus* to breach the structure in two places. The cost of repairs prevented the pier from extending any further than the 1,800ft already built, and once repairs had been made, Coatham Pier was reopened in 1875. The two entrance kiosks and the adjacent pavilion housing a roller-skating rink were built on the promenade whilst a second glazed pavilion was erected halfway along the pier.

Coatham Pier was besieged by frequent storms, the worst of which occurred on 22 October 1898. On that stormy day, the Finnish barque *Birger* was tossed into the pier, slicing the structure in two and causing a breach of 300ft. The ailing pier company was unable to meet the cost of repairs and the seaward end of the structure was demolished at the end of the year. In 1899, the Coatham Pier Company went bust and the main structure of the pier was eventually dismantled. Whilst the pier disappeared, only the entrance kiosks and shore end pavilion remained. The latter was demolished in 1910 but was replaced with a structure called the 'Glasshouse', later rebuilt as a theatre/cinema.

ABOVE: A 1950s view of what is often regarded as the UK's shortest pier. *(Richard Riding collection)*
BELOW: Coatham Pier pictured shortly before it was demolished during the winter of 1898-1899. *(Richard Riding collection)*

HORNSEA 1880-1897

Hornsea Pier probably holds the record for surviving in its completed state for the shortest period of time – barely six months. This small Yorkshire resort might well have ended up with two piers. Back in 1865, Joseph Wade, who had brought the railway to the town the year before, had founded the Hornsea Pier Company. Work on building the pier was slow and by 1871, only ten piles had been sunk and the project was abandoned. As Board of Trade orders to build piers lapsed after five years, Wade renewed his option and formed another company in 1873. Shortly afterwards, local businessman, Pierre du Gillon, put forward plans to build another pier half a mile from that of Wade's. Both piers received Board of Trade orders in 1877, but due to the legal costs of fighting his rival's plans, Gillon's company went bust in 1879.

Work had begun on Wade's pier, one of the last to be designed by Eugenius Birch, and despite problems with the contractors, the 1072ft structure was completed in May 1880. However, the pier fell into the hands of the official receiver a short time later, delaying its official opening. Disaster struck on the night of 28 October 1880 when a severe storm caused the vessel *Earl of Derby* to drift into the pier resulting in the loss of the pier head and 120ft of the neck. Despite this, the pier would open sporadically until 1896, being finally demolished the following year.

HYTHE 1881

Like a number of structures detailed in this book, Hythe Pier has been excluded from earlier books, as it was not considered a 'pleasure pier' as such. The earliest plans date back to 1870, but it was not until 1879 that work began. Designed by J. Wright, it was conceived to develop the existing steamer service across the River Test to Southampton Town Quay and was therefore a landing stage featuring a tollhouse, waiting room but no amusements. The final pile was driven in on 19 June 1880 and the 2100ft pier, its extensive length necessary to reach deep water even at low tide, was opened by the Mayor of Southampton on 1 January 1881. In 1894, a clubhouse for the Hythe Sailing Club was built at the pier head, and in 1896, re-planking and general repairs were carried out at a cost of £1,500.

Although plans for a railway to run the length of the 16ft wide pier had been suggested in 1870, it was not until 1909 that a track was laid to enable hand-propelled luggage trolleys to travel from one end to the other. A ticket office replaced the tollhouses in 1911. After World War 1, a refreshment room was opened in June 1919. In 1922, the baggage line was adapted to take passengers along a 2ft gauge and third-rail electric tramway, which was fenced off from the decking using British locomotives. During World War 2, ferry services continued normally; King George VI paid a visit to the pier prior to D-Day in 1944 and the structure largely escaped the attention of the enemy.

The pier entrance was modernised in the 1960s and more work was carried out on the pier head buildings during 1970-1977. A great deal of repair work totalling more than £500,000 was ordered during the 1980s. On 1 November 2003, the aggregate dredger MV *Donald Redford*, in the charge of a drunken skipper, collided with the mid-section of the pier causing a 75ft breach, which necessitated the replacement of four spans. This was repaired in record time and the pier was reopened for business on 7 January 2004.

LEFT: A post-war postcard view of Hythe Pier head, showing the 2ft gauge rail track on the right and the 300-passenger ferry *Hotspur II* berthed at the landing stage. *(Richard Riding collection)*

RAMSGATE MARINA 1881-1930

During its relatively short life, this pier was dogged by bad luck. In 1878, engineer Henry Robinson designed a simple 550ft promenade pier without a landing stage which was located a long way down the beach. Construction of the pier (known as Marina Pier, Iron Pier and Promenade Pier) was carried out by Head Wrightson of Stockton in 1879 and the official opening took place on 31 July 1881. Despite reasonably good patronage, the pier company encountered financial difficulties and was wound up in 1884 owing considerable sums to those responsible for the design and construction work.

The pier was auctioned that year and purchased by its builder for £2,000. Head Wrightson duly incorporated a 500-seat pavilion on the pier head, and in 1888, a short-lived switchback railway was erected along the entire length of the deck, dismantled barely three months later. The pier was sold to the Ramsgate Marina Pier & Lift Company in 1895 for £6,000 and was struck by the smack (a single-masted sailing boat for coasting or fishing) *British Queen* on 21 March 1895, damaging the structure. A fire also damaged the pier the following May. Facing large debts, the company was dissolved in 1904 and the pier was sold to a consortium for £600 in 1905.

ABOVE: Leith Trinity/Newhaven Chain Pier was the precursor of Brighton Chain Pier. *(Richard Riding collection)*

LEITH TRINITY CHAIN 1821-1898

Along with Portobello, Leith was one of two Scottish pleasure piers. There have been over 150 pier-like structures in Scotland, but most are classed as landing stages, river jetties and so on. Regarded as the precursor and template for Captain Sam Brown's second pier (Brighton Chain), Leith Trinity Chain Pier was opened on 14 August 1821. Costing £4,000, the pier consisted of three 209ft spans. Steamers from Dundee, Grangemouth and Stirling used the pier until the early 1850s. In later years, it fell into disuse and was finally destroyed by a storm on 18 October 1898, just two years after Brighton Chain met its end in similar circumstances.

PORTOBELLO 1871-1917

The 1250ft pier at Portobello was opened by the Lord Provost of Edinburgh in 1871. Designed by Thomas Bouch, it suffered greatly from persistent storm damage and collisions with steamers that ultimately led to the pier company's demise. The pier was later sold into private hands but was eventually demolished in 1917. Plans in 1939 for a second pier came to nothing. However, in 2005, a £35 million scheme to rejuvenate the town's 'tired and neglected' seafront were put forward, including provision for a new pier.

BELOW: An Edwardian postcard view of Portobello Pier c.1912. *(Richard Riding collection)*

The Pier, Portobello.

ABOVE: Ramsgate Marina Pier c.1900. *(Richard Riding collection)*

BELOW: One of many postcards published soon after Scarborough North Pier was destroyed by a severe storm on the night of 6 January 1905. *(Richard Riding collection)*

By 1909, the pier was in poor condition owing to lack of maintenance and changed hands in 1911. Additional amusements were added, including a joy wheel and a helter-skelter. During World War 1, the deteriorating pier lost its amusements and only attracted anglers. On 13 July 1918, an angler discarded a lit match towards the wooden pavilion with predictable consequences: the pier was completely wrecked. A drifting barge subsequently hit the structure and a mine exploded near the entrance and caused further damage in February 1919. In 1929, the Ministry of Transport acquired the festering pier and it was demolished during the summer of 1930.

SCARBOROUGH NORTH 1869-1905

Local banker J. W. Woodhall is credited as the driving force behind the building of Scarborough's pier. The Scarborough Promenade Pier Company Ltd gave the job of designing the 1,000ft structure to Eugenius Birch with the pier to be sited in the less popular north side of the resort. Construction began in 1866 and was initially put in the hands of J. E. Dowson. However, owing to his death, Head Wrightson completed the job and the pier was officially opened on 1 May 1869.

As with other Yorkshire piers, Scarborough was particularly susceptible to frequent storms, so much so that steamers were banned from calling due to frequent damage to the structure. In addition, various vessels hit the pier. In 1883, the steam trawler *Star* demolished several piles to be followed by a similar incident involving the steamer *Hardwick*. The band shelter was blown into the sea in December that year and the yacht *Escalpa* breached the structure.

In 1888, the pier company was wound up and the North Pier Company formed in an effort to repair and improve the ailing structure. A new entrance building replaced the earlier tollbooths and the pier head was widened to accommodate a pavilion. Whatever improvements the owners made, they failed to change the pier's fortune and the final straw came on the nights of 6-7 January 1905 when a severe storm flattened the structure leaving the pier head standing. Uninsured against such damage, the pier was never replaced, and although the marooned pavilion was demolished soon after, the entrance building stood as a reminder for another nine years.

SOUTHBOURNE 1888-1909

With a pier already existing at Bournemouth and another one planned for construction at nearby Boscombe, it was considered appropriate that up and coming Southbourne should have one too. The Southbourne Pier Company was set up and the pier's design went to local man Archibald Smith who was also working on Boscombe Pier. Southbourne's pier was a simple structure built of iron some 300ft long and 30ft wide. Apart from two tollbooths, the deck was free of buildings and amusements, its sole purpose to receive steamers. E. Howell of the Waterloo Foundry at Poole carried out the pier's construction at a cost of £4,000. The pier was officially opened on 2 August 1888 and the pleasure steamer *Lord Elgin* from nearby Bournemouth Pier commenced regular excursions between the two.

The pier prospered for its first twelve years but its fortune declined as the 19th century came to a close. On 28 December 1900, the pier fell victim to severe gales and was badly damaged. A knockout blow occurred on 3 January 1901 when another gale left the pier a twisted wreck. When the Southbourne Pier Company offered its wrecked pier to the local corporation, the offer was declined and the disabled pier was finally demolished in 1909.

WESTWARD HO! 1871-1880

Designed by J. W. Wilson for the Northam Burrows & Landing Pier Company, the Westward Ho! pier was short-lived and a victim of storms. Work started on the 600ft pier in the summer of 1870 and was in operation a year later. In October 1871, gales removed 150ft of the structure and a further gale in February 1880 caused sufficient damage to warrant the pier's demolition.

ABOVE: Southbourne Pier c.1901. *(Richard Riding collection)*

WITHERNSEA 1877-1903

Anthony Bannister was responsible for popularising Withernsea as a seaside resort and having brought the railway to the town in 1854 he formed the Withernsea Pier, Promenade, Gas & General Improvement Company in 1871 to introduce further tourist attractions, including a pleasure pier. Thomas Cargill, who had been responsible for Aldeburgh pier, was put in charge of structure's design and J. O. Gardiner was appointed as contractor. The cost of the project was £12,000. Even before the 1196ft pier was completed in August 1877, storms caused damage to the structure. On completion, the timber-decked pier was supported upon cast-iron piles screwed into the beach. Seating ran the entire length and the pier was entered via an imposing castellated building.

The official opening of the pier took place in 1878 and the venture was initially a financial success. However, on 28 October 1880, Withernsea was one of three Yorkshire piers badly damaged by storms when two damaged vessels hit the structure. One was the *Jabez*, which after hitting the pier, sank with the loss of all hands. The coal barge *Saffron* caused significant damage to the pier with a 200ft breach in the structure. Hardly had repairs taken place when the pier head was washed away on the night of 28 March 1883. On the night of 20 October 1890, the fishing smack *Genesta* ran into the unlit pier and removed more than half the remaining structure. On 22 March 1893, the *Henry Parr* hit the pier and sealed its fate forever. Only 50ft of the original pier remained and this disappeared in 1903. The castellated red brick entrance towers, something of a seafront folly, are all that remain of the pier today.

ABOVE: This Edwardian postcard of Withernsea Pier is deceptive because only 50ft of the pier structure was extant at the time. The entrance building is believed to have been modelled on Conway Castle. *(Richard Riding collection)*

BIBLIOGRAPHY

GENERAL BOOKS ON PIERS

Seaside Piers by Simon Adamson, published by Batsford (1977 and 1983).
Pavilions of the Sea by Cyril Bainbridge, published by Robert Hale (1986).
A Walk Across the Waves by Michael J. Burrell, published by Pear Tree Cottage Publications (1998).
Piers and Paddle Steamers in Camera by Pat Bushell, published by Quotes (1989).
Piers of Disaster by Martin Easdown, published by Hutton Press (1996).
A Guide to Collecting Seaside Pier Postcards by Martin Easdown and Richard Riding, self-published (2006).
British Piers photographs by Richard Fischer, published by Thames and Hudson (1987).
Piers & Seaside Towns – An Artist's Journey by Judith Greenbury, published by Sansom & Company (2001).
A Guide to British Piers (1st Ed) by Timothy Mickleburgh, published 1978 and reprinted 1979.
The Guide to British Piers (2nd Ed) by Timothy Mickleburgh, published by the Piers Information Bureau (1988).
The Guide to British Piers (3rd Ed) by Timothy Mickleburgh, published by the Piers Information Bureau (1998).
Glory Days – Piers by Timothy Mickleburgh, published by Ian Allan Publishing (1999).
Francis Frith's Piers Photographic Memories text by Timothy Mickleburgh, published by the Frith Book Company (2000).
Oh! What a Lovely Pier by Daphne Mitchell, published by QueenSpark Market Books (1996).

BOOKS ON SPECIFIC PIERS

Bangor Pier Centenary 1896-1996: A History of the Pier published by the City of Bangor Council (1996).
The Brighton Chain Pier In Memoriam by John George Bishop, published by J. G. Bishop (1896).
The North Pier Blackpool 1863-1913 published by Blackpool North Pier Company (1913).
The Story of Southend Pier by Alderman H.N. Bride, published by Southend-on-Sea Corporation (*c.*1950).
Palace Pier Brighton by Albert Bullock and Peter Medcalf, published by Alan Sutton (1999).
A Necessary Monument: An Illustrated History of Clevedon Pier by Jeremy Burman, published by Oxford Polytechnic (1976).
Southend Pier and Its Story: 1829-1835-1935 by John Wm Burrows, published by John A. Barrows & Sons (1936).
Years of Piers: Memories of St Annes Pier on its Centenary by Paul Cantrell, published by Handbook Publishing (1985).
Penarth Pier 1894-1994 by Phil Carradice, published by Baron Birch for Quotes (1994).
Striding Boldly: The Story of Clevedon Pier by Nigel Coombes, published by the Clevedon Pier Trust Ltd (1995).
The North Pier Story Blackpool by Cyril Critchlow, published by the author (2002).
Piering into the Past by Mike Davies, published by the Friends of the Old Pier Society (2002).

A Potted History of Birnbeck Pier and Island with a Peep into the Future published by the Friends of the Old Pier Society in (2000).
A Tale of Three Piers by Jon De Jonge, published by Lancashire County Books (1993).
The Longest Pier in the World: A Pictorial History of Southend Pier 1830-1986 by Peggy Dowie and Ken Crowe, published by Friends of Southend Pier Museum (1987).
A Century of Iron: A History of Southend's Iron Pier 1889-1989 by Peggy Dowie and Ken Crowe, published by Friends of Southend Pier Museum (1989).
Times of a Troubled Pier (Scarborough) by Martin Easdown, published by Marlinova (2005).
Victoria's Golden Pier (Folkestone) by Martin Easdown, published by Marlin Publications (1998).
A Fateful Finger of Iron (Ramsgate) by Martin Easdown, published by Michaels Bookshop (2006).
Southend Pier by Martin Easdown, published by Tempus Publishing Limited (2007).
Piers of Kent by Martin Easdown, published by Tempus Publishing Limited (2007).
Herne Bay's Piers by Harold Gough, published by Pierhead Publications (2002).
Walking on Water: Brighton West Pier Story by Fred Gray, published by Brighton West Pier Trust (1998).
The War Story of Southend by A. P. Herbert, published by the County Borough of Southend (1945).
The Story of Hastings Pier by Gaby Koppel & Mike Barron, published by Hastings Pier Company (1982).
Piers of the Isle of Wight by Marian Lane, published by the Isle of Wight Council (1996).
Clevedon Pier by K. Mallory, published by Redcliffe Press (1981).
Cleethorpes Pier and Promenade by Timothy Mickleburgh, published by North East Lincolnshire Council (2000).
Piers of the North by Timothy Mickleburgh, published (1998).
Threatened Piers by Timothy Mickleburgh, published by Piers Information Bureau (1990).
Threatened Piers: The Saga Continues by Tim Mickleburgh, published by the Piers Information Bureau (1992).
Clyde Piers: A Pictorial Record by John Monteith & Ian McCrorie, published by Inverclyde District Libraries (1982).
Grandeur & Decay: A Salvaged History of Clevedon Pier by Paul Newman, published by Engart Press (1981).
The History of Cromer Pier by Christopher Pipe, published by Poppyland Publishing (1998).
The Romance of the Old Chain Pier at Brighton by Ernest Ryman, published by Dyke Publications (1996).
Seaview Pier: The Case History by Adrian Searle, published by Isle of Wight County Press (1981).
The Story of Southend Pier by E. W. Shepherd, published by Egon Publishers Ltd (1979).
Years of Piers and Discovering Skegness by Edmena Simpson, published by Paul Cantrell (1992).
Bangor Pier 1896-1988 by Ian Skidmore, published by Gwasg Carreg Gwaich (1998).
The End of the Pier Book: A Pictorial History of Redcar and Coatham Piers by Peter Sotheran, published by A. A. Sotheran Ltd. (1996).
Southend-on-Sea: The Longest Pleasure Pier in the World; published by Southend-on-Sea Council (*c.* 2000).
Birnbeck Pier: A Short History by Stan Terrell, published by the North Somerset Museum Service (1986).

Skegness Pier by Albert E. Thompson (*c.* 1988).

Hythe Pier and Ferry: A History by Alan Titheridge, published by Itchen Printers (1996; originally published 1981).

Palace Pier by Keith Waterhouse, published by Sceptre (2003).

The Harbours and Piers of Ventnor 1843-1988 published by Ventnor & District Local History Society (1988).

Glimpses of Bognor Regis Pier 1865-1990 by Paul Wells and Sylvia Endacott, published by S. Endacott (1990 reprinted in 1998 in new format with some different pictures).

Worthing Pier: A History by Dr Sally White, published by Worthing Museum (1996).

Teignmouth Pier – A Pictorial History by Viv Wilson, self-published (2003).

PIER RAILWAYS & TRAMWAYS

Southend Pier Railway by K. A. Frost, published by Peter R. Davis (1965).

Blackpool North Pier Tramway by Alison Orchard, published by Lancastrian Transport Publications (1992).

The Piers, Tramways and Railways at Ryde by R. J. Maycock & R. Silsbury, published by The Oakwood Press (2005).

PIERS & SEASIDE ARCHITECTURE

Seaside Architecture by Kenneth Lindley, published by Hugh Evelyn (1973).

The People's Palaces by Dr Lynn F. Pearson, published by Barracuda Books (1991).

Piers and Other Seaside Architecture by Dr Lynn F. Pearson, published by Shire Publications Ltd. (2002).

ACKNOWLEDGEMENTS

In putting together the potted histories of the 100 or so piers covered in this volume, the authors owe a great debt to Tim Mickleburgh and Martin Easdown, Hon. Vice-President and Archivist respectively of the National Piers Society, who are the pioneers in researching the history of our piers. Tim Mickleburgh's Guide to British Piers, now in its third edition, has been invaluable in the production of this book, and Martin Easdown has kindly read through the manuscript and weeded out any inaccuracies. Any remaining errors are the authors' alone.

The authors are grateful to the following for their assistance: Mike Evans and Lindsay Jones at English Heritage, Peter Waller for getting the ball rolling, Nick Grant and book editor Jay Slater at Ian Allan Publishing, and Mick Willis and Joyce Barrett, both formerly at Aerofilms.

The National Piers Society was founded in 1979 under the late Sir John Betjeman and others. Richard Riding has edited the Society's quarterly journal *PIERS* since 2002, his predecessor for many years being Martin Easdown. *PIERS* is another source for much of the material published here and anyone wishing to get more involved with the pier world can join the Society by visiting its website at www.piers.co.uk. Specific books on piers are few and far between but a comprehensive listing of those published to date can be found in the bibliography, together with other useful and more general reference sources.

All the aerial photographs in this book (unless indicated otherwise) were sourced from the Aerofilms collection of aerial photographs, the UK's first commercial aerial photographic library, founded in 1919 and wound up in 2006. In 2007, this archive of some one million images was purchased by English Heritage and its partners, The Royal Commission on the Ancient and Historical Monuments of Scotland and the Royal Commission on the Ancient and Historical Monuments of Wales, thus preserving it for the nation. These photos have therefore been reproduced by kind permission of English Heritage and RCAHMW and are © English Heritage. NMR and © Crown: Royal Commission on the Ancient and Historical Monuments of Wales. Photos from other sources are credited in the text.

1814	**Ryde**
1821	Leigh Trinity Chain (demolished 1898)
1823	Brighton Chain (demolished 1896)
1830	Southend (1) (demolished 1887)
	Walton-on-the-Naze Old (demolished 1880)
1832	Herne Bay (1) (demolished 1862)
1835	Sheerness (demolished 1971)
1838	Deal (1) (demolished 1857)
1840	Weymouth Commercial (demolished 1933)
1846	**Lowestoft South**
1853	**Great Yarmouth Wellington**
1855	Margate Jetty (demolished 1978)
1858	Gt Yarmouth Britannia (1) (demolished 1899)
1860	**Southport**
1861	Bournemouth (1) (demolished 1876)
	Southsea Clarence
1862	**Worthing**
1863	**Blackpool North**
1864	Deal (2) (demolished 1940)
	Ryde Victoria IOW (demolished 1924)
1865	**Aberystwyth**
	Bognor Regis
	Lytham (demolished 1924)
1866	**Brighton West**
1867	**Teignmouth**
	Weston-super-Mare Birnbeck/Old

	New Brighton (demolished 1977)
	Rhyl (demolished 1973)
1868	**Blackpool Central**
1869	**Clevedon**
	Saltburn
	Douglas IOM (demolished 1894)
	Morecambe Central (demolished 1992)
	Scarborough (demolished 1905)
1870	**Eastbourne**
	Hunstanton (demolished 1978)
1871	**Clacton-on-Sea**
	Walton-on-the-Naze New
	Portobello (demolished 1917)
	Westward Ho! (demolished 1880)
1872	**Hastings**
	Ventnor IOW (demolished 1993)
1873	Herne Bay (2)
	Redcar (demolished 1981)
	Cleethorpes
	Coatham (demolished 1899)
1876	Aldeburgh (demolished c.1890)
	Yarmouth IOW
1877	**Llandudno**
	Withernsea (demolished 1903)
1878	**Sandown IOW**
1879	**Paignton**

	Southsea South Parade (1)
	Pegwell Bay (demolished 1885)
1880	**Bournemouth (2)**
	Totland Bay IOW
	Hornsea (demolished 1897)
1881	**Hythe**
	Skegness
	Ramsgate (demolished 1930)
	Seaview Chain IOW (demolished 1952)
1884	Plymouth (demolished 1953)
1885	**St Anne's-on-Sea**
1886	**Ramsey Queens IOM**
1887	Alum Bay IOW (demolished 1950s)
1888	Folkestone (demolished 1954)
	Lee-on-Solent (demolished 1958)
	Southbourne (demolished 1909)
1889	**Boscombe**
	Southend-on-Sea (2)
1890	Shanklin IOW (demolished 1993)
1891	St Leonards (demolished 1958)
1892	Southhampton Royal (derelict by 1990s)
1893	**Blackpool South**
	Dover (demolished 1927)
1895	**Penarth**
	Rhos-on-Sea (demolished 1954)
	Torquay

	Beaumaris
1896	**Bangor**
	Swanage
	Morecambe West End (demolished 1978)
1897	Tenby (demolished 1953)
1898	**Walton-on-the-Naze New (2)**
	Mumbles
1899	**Brighton Palace**
	Herne Bay (3)
1900	Southwold (incorporated into new pier 2001)
	Colwyn Bay
1901	**Cromer**
	Minehead (demolished 1940)
	Gt Yarmouth Britannia (2)
1902	Cowes Victoria IOW (demolished 1965)
	Aberavon (not a pleasure pier from c.1940)
1903	**Lowestoft Claremont**
1904	**Weston-Super-Mare Grand**
1905	**Felixstowe** and **Falmouth Prince of Wales**
1908	**Southsea South Parade**
1910	**Fleetwood**
1933	**Weymouth Commercial (2)**
1939	Weymouth Bandstand (demolished 1986)
1957	**Deal (3)**
1961	**Southsea Clarence (2)**
2001	**Southwold (new)**

The graphs do not include piers built before 1838 or after 1910. Surviving piers are in bold type. Piers that were greatly extended to become new structures are in brackets.

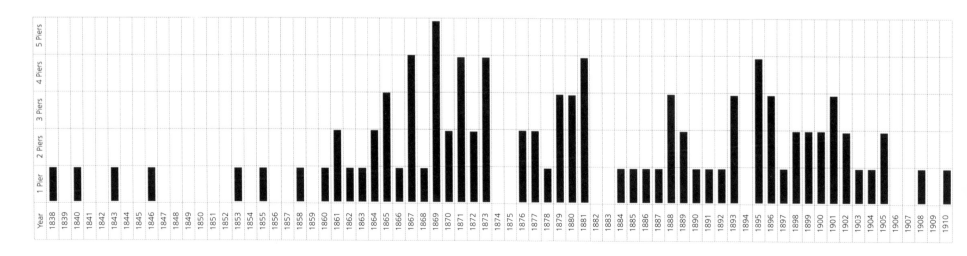